SHRINK-PROOF YOUR LIFE

Top Ten Ways to Stay off the Therapist's Couch

Peter Allman, MA

Copyright © 2016 Peter Allman, M.A.

All rights reserved. No part of this book may be reproduced, stored, or transmitted by any means—whether auditory, graphic, mechanical, or electronic—without written permission of both publisher and author, except in the case of brief excerpts used in critical articles and reviews. Unauthorized reproduction of any part of this work is illegal and is punishable by law.

ISBN: 978-1-4834-5572-3 (sc)
ISBN: 978-1-4834-5573-0 (e)

Library of Congress Control Number: 2016912347

Because of the dynamic nature of the Internet, any web addresses or links contained in this book may have changed since publication and may no longer be valid. The views expressed in this work are solely those of the author and do not necessarily reflect the views of the publisher, and the publisher hereby disclaims any responsibility for them.

Any people depicted in stock imagery provided by Thinkstock are models, and such images are being used for illustrative purposes only.
Certain stock imagery © Thinkstock.

Lulu Publishing Services rev. date: 07/26/2016

For Mom and Dad

Table of Contents

Introduction.. ix
Very, Very Important Preface: It's always an inside job. xv

Chapter One: Name Your Issue... 1
Chapter Two: Resolve Conflicts 11
Chapter Three: Let Go and Forgive 22
Chapter Four: Accept What Is (and Be Willing to Have a Plan B) 31
Chapter Five: Parent Yourself 41
Chapter Six: Get Outside Yourself..51
Chapter Seven: Practice Being Non-attached 62
Chapter Eight: Talk to Someone 72
Chapter Nine: See Your Thoughts.. 82
Chapter Ten: Use Healthy Coping Strategies 92

Epilogue... 99

Introduction

There is no escaping normal. It is normal for life to sometimes be like a rodeo. You're on that bronco and you know that at some point you are going to be bucked off. Have you learned to land safely? Are you always getting injured? Do you blame the bucking bronco? Down the road, do you get back on the bronco that bucked you, or do you find a new event better suited for you? Or, are you now in the stands watching?

Most of us are creatures of habit. This is normal. But some habits—specifically our thinking patterns—can be unhealthy. We might stay in the same life-sucking job or in a dysfunctional relationship. We might have problems with authority. We might have strained connections to family members. Basically it's the same rodeo. We get bucked off again, and again, and again.

To paraphrase Isaac Newton: an object in motion will stay in motion unless acted upon by an outside force. This is easy to see in the physical world. For example, the ball will keep rolling until a wall stops it or someone picks it up. It is also true in our internal world. A thought—"an object"—will go and go and go until we interrupt our own thought process or something happens like a car swerving into our lane, which makes us quickly change our thoughts. We will think incessantly about how our boss treated us, pick apart something our spouse said, or replay a conversation with one of our children's teachers.

Sometimes our thoughts are so negative that we create disharmony in our relationships, don't perform well at work, or treat ourselves in a harmful way. In these circumstances, the "outside force" may be something severe, like a divorce, loss of a job, being confronted by a loved one about an addiction, a life-threatening illness, or a therapist's couch.

I wrote this book to be your "outside force." *Shrink Proof Your Life* will help you break out of a negative habit or a suffocating situation. It will help you become more aware of the thoughts that can lead you to "heaven" or "hell." It will help you with the normal events—the bucking broncos—that happen in your life. And, it will help you spiral upward to a healthier, more joyful existence…off the therapist's couch where you become your own counselor.

I have been a psychotherapist for more than twenty years. I have noticed a pattern of thoughts that is common to many people and that leads to behaviors that bring people into my office. Seeing that pattern led me to write this book. Now, two disclaimers. First, people will still need therapy. These chapters are not enough help for a person with a major mental health disorder. Clinical depression, schizophrenia, bipolar disorder, and dissociative identity disorder are a few of the diagnoses that need more of an intervention than this book. People with disorders like autism, Asperger's syndrome, or fetal alcohol syndrome need more assistance than this book offers. People who have experienced sexual, physical, emotional abuse and other tragic circumstances, will also benefit from counseling.

Second, a professional counselor is beneficial even if you do not have a major mental health disorder. The therapist can add a new perspective or tweak an existing one, be a neutral mediator, bring validation to your life, or simply listen to your story. But, with the help of this book, you can definitely spend less time on the therapist's couch. You will have fewer out-of-pocket expenses and fewer co-pays to make during the year. And, if you have already been to counseling, this book will provide reminders or new strategies that will keep you from going back.

I tell my clients that my ultimate job is to equip them to be their own counselors. I need to help them learn and integrate therapeutic strategies, so they can have healthier and more functional thoughts. If they do so, they will continue to make better choices—which will create happier lives. You will see the "bucking bronco" for what it is and choose to not jump on anymore—or at least take responsibility when you get bucked off.

My job is to share therapeutic metaphors and images for clients to use across all sorts of situations. I will not be there when the bucking bronco shows up. I will share these metaphors and images with you because I won't be there with you either when you get bucked off the horse.

In each chapter, I write about the power of your thoughts and challenge you to be aware of them. I believe our thoughts create our reality. If you do not believe this, try a little experiment. Stop and notice the weather outside. Is it sunny, cloudy, windy, calm, cool, or hot? Now create a negative thought about the weather. For example, "I don't like the wind—I have to stay inside instead of playing golf today." "I wish it weren't so hot. I have to drive to the store, and it's going to be 110 degrees in my car." Or, "Bummer. It's calm and cool outside and I'm stuck at work." How do these thoughts make you feel? Annoyed, disturbed, sad, mad? You created those states of being by having those specific thoughts.

Now, continue the experiment and flip your thoughts. "Oh, it's windy. Instead of playing golf, I'll take the dogs on a long walk." (Or, "I'll finish the painting project in the basement.") "It's another hot summer day. I'm glad my car has air conditioning." Finally, "It's a beautiful calm and cool day. I'm going to eat lunch outside today." How do these thoughts make you feel? Satisfied, happy, content, grateful? It is exactly the same scenario outside, and you did the "inside job" of creating positive and healthier thoughts. You, and you alone, have created a happier state of being. It is always an inside job.

In order to understand that our thoughts create our reality, you must first be able to see your thoughts. Be an interested observer of your thoughts. Notice them. If they make you unhappy, communicate and try to resolve an unhappy circumstance, or create new thoughts that lead you to a more peaceful place. Change your thoughts. They are merely thoughts. You have thousands, if not millions of thoughts a day. You created them. You have the power to create healthier ones. Albert Einstein said, "The world we have created is a product of our thinking. It cannot be changed without changing our thinking."

One of the leading thinkers in the 19th century and the first educator to teach a psychology course in the United States, was William James. He wrote, "The greatest weapon against stress is our ability to choose one thought over another." I had a client who was trying to teach his adult child an important life lesson. The 24-year-old son was defensive and did not want to change his way of life. The dad "saw" one of his own thoughts that, if he shared it, could have shamed the adult child. The dad had learned to be aware of his thoughts and choose which ones to manifest. He let go of the shaming thought and did not create more stress in the interaction with his son. He chose to create a healthier thought and then communicate that thought to his son.

Incorporating spirituality in our lives—believing in a God or Higher Being—helps us heal and transcend many earthly issues. Being aware of our thoughts, observing them and changing them can be helped by having a spiritual practice or outlook. That doesn't necessarily mean going to church or joining a religion. I have two views of religion. One is negative and the other is positive.

The following statement reinforces the negative paradigm of religion; "Religion is for those who are scared of hell. Spirituality is for those who have been to hell." This is the negative view of people who go to church as some sort of insurance policy so they won't go to hell. These people tend to claim their religion, but not necessarily live the tenets.

The following statement depicts the positive paradigm of religion: "Religion is the container where spirituality can occur." That is the positive view, where churches teach, model, and create programs centering on love, tolerance, justice, and other values that help humankind heal and evolve.

When I include spirituality in this book, it is from many different faiths and teachers. No religion has the monopoly on truth. You will read truths from Jesus, Buddha, Gandhi, Rumi, Native American religion, and Einstein who incorporated spirituality and science. Or, we could all just follow this simple truth stated by the Dalai Lama: "My religion is kindness."

You want to change. You want to grow and evolve into a better person. This book can help you. Gandhi said, "Be the change you want to see in the world." When you do this, then others may notice and they may ask why you are so happy. Since they asked, you can teach them these truths. This process will help solidify the truths in your mind and make your new practices new habits.

Here's my last piece of advice before you journey into *Shrink Proof Your Life*. You will think about the strategies and try them out. A typical reaction is to think, "This is hard." Be aware of this thought and please change it to, "This is a practice." If you say it will be hard, guess what? It will always be hard. By contrast, everyone can practice a new skill. If you want to get better at bowling, do you say, "This is hard"? No, you say to yourself, "I am going to practice." One learns by doing. .) Henry Ford was correct when he said, "Whether you believe you can do a thing or not, you are right."

In each chapter, you will read about therapeutic conversations that occurred in my office. Clients agree and resonate with new insights. When they realize they need to practice these new ways of seeing the world (thoughts), they say, "This will be hard." Of course, I challenge them to change 'hard' to 'practice.' (Every client's name has been changed to preserve confidentiality).

Growth usually doesn't occur in quantum leaps. Coral islands are built from skeletons of corals and numerous other animals associated with corals. The organic material of billions of these animals has slowly, gradually, incrementally formed the islands.

Our positive changes will come incrementally. Practice, practice, and practice some more. Practice is power. Practice does not create perfect. Practice creates permanent. You have had many years of thinking and living a certain way. We are all creatures of habit. That is normal. You will slowly create new neuropathways in your brain when you practice these new skills. Then, the next time your spouse or partner says something inappropriate to you, it will be easier to resolve the conflict (Chapter 2), let go and forgive (Chapter 3), be willing (Chapter 4). I think you are seeing the pattern.

There is a story from long ago about an old monk who was going on a pilgrimage to the monastery of a wise Buddhist monk which was at the foot of a sacred mountain. The monk had been traveling for months and he had grown weak. One day he gazed upward and saw the majestic mountain in the distance. There was an old woman by the road who was working in the field. He asked her, "Excuse me, please tell me how much longer I must walk before reaching the monastery?" The woman just looked at him, grunted and returned to her work. The old monk repeated the question many, many times, but still there was no answer.

Thinking that the woman must be deaf, he decided to continue his walk. After he had taken a few dozen steps, he heard the woman call out to him. "Two more days—it will take you two more days." Very surprised, the monk yelled, "I thought you were deaf. Why didn't you answer my question earlier?" The woman replied, "You asked the question while you were standing still. I had to see how fast your pace was, how determined your walk."

How soon you leave the therapist's couch and become your own counselor will be determined by your pace and how determined you are. Forge ahead, and with practice, you will reach your destination.

Very, Very Important Preface: It's always an inside job.

There is a story that a reporter once asked Albert Einstein what he thought was the most important question of the day. Einstein wanted to honor the question, so he asked to think about it and then get back to the reporter. Soon, he responded by saying: each and every person needs to answer for him or herself, is the Universe a friendly or hostile place?

How would you answer that question? I believe the Universe is a friendly place. In fact, I think it is conspiring for your benefit. The 13th century Persian poet and Sufi mystic Rumi wrote, "Live life as if everything is rigged in your favor." That is exciting. That is hopeful. It is an important way to help you stay off the therapist's couch and be your own counselor.

Obviously, there are hostile people in the world, and pockets of hostility. That does not mean the Universe is hostile. The key is to stay away from those hostile situations.

We are here to learn lessons. We are here to heal. We are here to clear karma. Whatever your name for your higher being is: the Universe, God, the Force, Consciousness, or Great Spirit, that energy and Intelligence is helping you grow and evolve. Since most of us don't learn early and quickly, our lessons become more difficult. That does not mean the Universe is hostile. In fact, God (or your name for a Higher Being) loves you so much and wants so much for you to learn your lessons, that a bigger fire is lit beneath you to wake you up.

Because of this truth, here is another very, very important concept: nothing happens *to* you, everything happens *for* you.

That is a 180 for most of us.

If you think the Universe is hostile, you will think things happen *to* you. This will make you a victim—which will further "prove" the Universe is hostile.

If you think the Universe is both friendly and hostile, when "bad" things happen to you, this will "prove" the Universe is hostile. Then, when "good" things happen to you, this will "prove" the Universe is also friendly. You will live a bipolar-like life.

When you believe the experiences of your life happen *to* you, life becomes meaningless, random, and a sense of boredom can occur. An ever-present anger and low level of depression can be present. You will feel like a victim. When you believe the experiences are *for* you, then there is meaning and purpose to life. We wake up and see the messages within the experiences. We learn, grow, and evolve into our Better Self.

Everything that happens is offered as a gift or a healing. We will not have this perspective unless we have eyes to see this truth. We need to be more conscious, more awake, more aware of our thoughts. Never have the attitude, "poor me." Try to have the attitude, "how can I see this as good for me"?

There is a wonderful story that illuminates a new way of seeing the world. This story is told in different ways in *Sadhana: A Way to God,* by Anthony de Mello, *Way of the Peaceful Warrior,* by Dan Millman, and the movie, *Charlie Wilson's War.* Here is an amalgamation of these three sources.

There is an ancient Chinese story of an old farmer who only had one horse and one son to help him on his farm. One day the horse escaped and all the farmer's neighbors felt sad for him. They told him they were sorry for his bad luck. The wise farmer said, "Good luck? Bad luck? Who know? We shall see." A couple of days later, the horse came back with five wild mares. This time the neighbors congratulated the farmer on his good luck. His wise reply was, "Good luck? Bad luck? Who knows? We shall see." A week later, his son was taming one of the wild horses and got bucked off and broke his leg. Again, the neighbors expressed their sadness, and thought this was very bad luck. The farmer responded the same way, "Good luck? Bad luck? Who knows? We shall see." Some weeks later, the army came through his small village and rounded up all the young men to go off to war. When they found the farmer's son with a broken leg, they left him behind.

This story shines a light on how most of us live in a short-sighted way. We haven't learned or practiced fully trusting God/Higher Power/

the Universe, so we become bipolar. "That's bad." "That's good." "That's bad." "That's good." As Shakespeare wrote in *Hamlet,* "There is nothing either good or bad, but thinking makes it so."

It is all for our benefit. It is all for our awakening. It is all for us to see our wounds so we can heal them. It is for us to more fully merge into the Divine.

Here is the third of the very, very important concepts. With everything that happens, say to yourself: "Bless him (her), change me." The other person is showing up to help you see your lesson. Learn your lesson sooner than later so he or she doesn't have to keep showing up in that particular way.

For example, if you have a problem with boundaries, I promise you that people will often show up in your life and ask a lot of you. Bless that person for awakening you to the truth that you need to say no. Then change yourself and say no!

If you are living with an alcoholic husband, I promise you that he will keep coming home drunk to awaken you to the truth that you are co-dependent, or too passive. Then change yourself and join Al-Anon, and let him know that you are leaving the marriage unless drastic changes occur.

If you have problems with patience, I promise you that you will consistently have slow drivers in front of you on the road, and you will pick the slowest line at the grocery story. Bless the driver and cashier, and change yourself. Pray, meditate, smile, or laugh at the absurdity of getting mad at these small events.

The old saying is true: Everyone comes into your life for a reason, a season, or a lifetime. They come into our life *for* us. There is a reason. So bless them because the Universe wants you to learn a particular lesson. Then change yourself so you can grow into your Better Self.

The Universe is a friendly place. This belief will help you see that nothing happens to you. Everything happens for you. And then you will be able to live the prayer: bless the other person, and change me. It's always an inside job.

When working with his clients, psychologist Carl Jung noticed significant and meaningful coincidences that helped his clients grow and heal. These coincidences were not caused or created by the clients. He called this phenomena "synchronicity." This is what happens when you are aware the Universe is working for you. For example, you "coincidently" run into an old friend or acquaintance. He or she tells you something you really needed to hear to help you on your journey. You did not create this interaction. God created this "chance" meeting because the Universe is friendly and conspiring to help you.

A pastor had a poster of a beautiful picture of an ocean with two dolphins leaping from the water and forming a yin yang symbol. The word Synchronicity was written at the bottom of the poster. A young person came into the pastor's office and thought the picture was a travel poster and asked, "Where is Synchron city?" The pastor laughed and said, "It is the place where you and God live as one. This is where you will clearly see the signs to help you find direction, meaning, and purpose in your life."

For some of you reading this right now, you have this awareness about how the Universe works. For others, it may be completely new. Some of us have this awareness in our minds but it may take a while to get to our hearts. Or maybe sometimes we forget about these truths, especially when times are tough. Awakening or enlightenment is not a switch that stays on or off. The more we practice bringing this awareness and truth to our minds and especially to our hearts, the more joy and fun we will experience—and less time on the therapist's couch. Remember to treat yourself as you would want to treat your children or any other beloved person: with patience and love. You are worth it!

Chapter One

Name Your Issue

Richard came into my office dressed to the nines: lightly starched Brooks Brothers white shirt, burgundy silk tie, and a classic pinstripe suit. His hair was perfectly coiffed—not a hair out of place. His black shoes were shined as if he were in the military. He was 38 years old, and the public relations director for a large insurance company.

After the preliminary greeting and small talk, I asked Richard to catch me up and tell me why he scheduled this meeting. He told me his wife said he was too anxious. She was tired of him biting his nails until they bled. She was tired of him not being able to sleep and not coming to bed when she did. She was tired of him never sitting still.

I told Richard that his wife had just answered my question. I was more interested in his perspective.

He smiled and said he probably agreed with his wife.

Richard had half-heartedly named his issue. "How long have you suffered from anxiety?" I asked him.

"Oh man," Richard said, "probably since 6th grade,"

"Why do you think it started then?"

"I don't know. Maybe school work got harder? My mom also moved us to another area of town."

Richard and I talked about the nature of an anxious mind, strategies he had used to deal with it, and relaxation strategies for him to practice. Richard had made some progress, but he was still very anxious and continued to do the behaviors his wife had talked about.

By our fourth session, Richard felt much more comfortable with counseling, and trust had developed in our relationship. We talked about work, parenting, marriage, spirituality, and his hobbies. At the end of this session when we were winding down the counseling, Richard said, "Pete, did I ever share with you that I was molested by a neighbor when I was in elementary school?"

Now Richard had named the real issue. He shared it at a time when we could not talk about it—at the end of our session. He was unconsciously testing the waters. I remained calm. "No, Richard, you have never told me that. I am very sorry. Can we talk about that during our next session?"

"Yes. I'm sorry I didn't tell you sooner. I don't think about it often."

Unconsciously, he thought about it all the time. The sexual abuse sits in his psyche like an infected boil. As a child, his life had been out of control. Richard dresses meticulously to try and show himself and the world he now has everything under control. He did such an excellent job of presenting a good front that he was promoted at a young age to do exactly that—to present a good front on behalf of the insurance company as head of public relations.

Richard was devoting all of his time and energy to dealing with his internal issue in the external world. He was not doing any work in his internal world. This is common. Most people are afraid of bringing their issue to light because they think it will overwhelm them. The exact opposite is true. If they bring the issue to the light, it will lose power. Even something as big as sexual abuse will lose its power when it is named and brought to the light.

For example, if a small child is afraid there is a boogie man in her closet, the parent opens the closet door, turns on the light, and the child can see no one is there to harm her. Then she might say the boogie man is under her bed. The parent brings a flashlight, shines the light and she can see no one is there.

The same is true with our interior work. When we repress an issue, it is left in the dark. Things are scarier in the dark. Then we try to numb the pain by drinking, working long hours, or watching hours and hours of television. As J.K. Rowling wrote in *Harry Potter and the Goblet of Fire*, "Numbing the pain for a while will only make it worse when you finally feel it." If we bring the issue up to the light, we feel relieved, lighter, and the healing can begin because now we can now deal with the issue.

When clients gain a new insight or name their issue, I tell them that they are now halfway toward resolving the problem. The other half is the new thoughts, behaviors, and coping strategies that replace the old, negative ones. You can't work on a new way of being in the world if you don't know what your unhealthy ways that are keeping you stuck!

Richard and I would never have made significant progress if he hadn't named and shared the real issue. His anxiety was symptomatic of the sexual trauma he experienced. My job is to help the client figure out the core issue so he or she can deal with the root of the problem. If we only deal with the symptoms, the root will keep producing symptoms.

As Gilda, the good witch told Dorothy waving her wand at the yellow brick road, "It's always best to start at the beginning," There is a rhyming strategy which helps people "start at the beginning" and learn their life lessons. Name it (the issue), claim it, tame it, to reframe it. Once you name the issue, then you can own it, then deal with it, and ultimately see how the problem itself and its resolution have actually helped you grow and become more whole.

In the counseling world, moving an issue from the unconscious to the conscious is called insight. Insight is the beginning of the sacred journey toward health and wholeness. The process includes many discoveries. Based on all the aspects of your life, it is a process of re-discovery: seeing how the issue got triggered in your workplace, with family, by friends, driving your car, or waiting in the grocery line. Implementing the truths from the following chapters, you can watch and de-power the internal rollercoaster of emotions, instead of jumping on and feeling off-balance the rest of the day.

I once knew a man named Sam. Everyone in Sam's family knew he was an alcoholic. Sam could never admit he had a problem. His defense mechanisms were strong and he had an answer for everything presented to him. "The boss is an ass." "I don't have a bottle of Jack in my desk drawer." "I am not living on the streets." These responses were true, but they were only half of the truth. He was also on his third and final warning at work. His wife was always mad at him, and he woke up often with a hangover.

It is no accident that the very first step of the Alcoholics Anonymous twelve step program is "We admit we are powerless over alcohol and our lives have become unmanageable." This is naming the issue. This is bringing the issue to the light. This is naming it, by which to claim it, so to tame it, and then reframe it. It is also no accident that everyone introduces themselves at every AA meeting by saying, "I'm (person's name), and I'm an alcoholic." That is naming the issue.

When I am working with an adolescent, the parent(s) also need to be present for many of the sessions. In our first session, I ask the teen to help me and tell me what's going on in his or her life, and why he or she thinks we have all gathered together. Typically, the teen tells me half of the story. And, typically, the teen blames teachers, parents, siblings, and school administrators.

I have found the best strategy—the best metaphor—to help the teen name the issue and tell me the whole story. Since the teen is already driving a car, or soon will be driving a car, I use the metaphor of a car on a road. I tell the teen I want him or her to be in the driver's seat of his or her car— his life. I also tell teens that what's normal is for the parent to be on the passenger seat: watching, and making sure the teen makes good decisions and stays on the road.

If the teen starts moving toward the shoulder of the road, the parent needs to say, "Wake up, Ethan. Turn back onto the road, or I will (metaphorically) hit the brakes!" I then tell the teen that this is good parenting, and the parents' ultimate job is to make sure their adolescent child does not end up in the ditch.

I tell the teen that I want him to have the power in his life. I tell him if he is making good decisions and doing well in his life—staying on the road—I will turn to his parents and tell them that I believe they can relax, not parent so much, because Ethan is doing well.

Every teen loves to hear this. Then I ask the $64,000 question: Ethan, where is your "car?" Solidly on the road? On the shoulder? A couple of tires on the shoulder? In the ditch?

Usually, the teen will now start the process of naming the issue. He might say two tires are on the shoulder. I will ask him to name the behaviors of those two tires. He might say, "I have a couple of F's in school, and I cuss too much at my parents."

I then ask the parents to say where they believe Ethan's car is. Hopefully, their answer is pretty close to his answer. The parents and the teen have to agree upon where the "car" is before counseling can continue. That is our roadmap. Most importantly, this is the roadmap for the teen to find his way out of counseling. Therapy then can begin because the issue(s) have been named.

If we don't name our issue, projection will probably occur. Projection is when we do not name and own our problem, but the problem is still alive and kicking inside of us. These thoughts and feelings created by the issue have to go somewhere so we ascribe them to somebody else. So, in fact, our eyes show us what we believe, not what we see.

> Our eyes show us what we believe, not what we see.

For example, let's say I wake up angry. I don't name the anger and I arrive Monday morning at the psychology class I teach at a local college. Let's further say the students don't participate in the class discussion and are not smiling and acknowledging me during the lecture. Before we take our first break, I ask the students why they are so angry this morning. They respond by telling me that they are not angry, they are all tired.

I projected my unconscious anger in me on to the students. I made my issue their issue. Luckily they didn't own my projection and communicated what was really their reality.

The author Anais Nin wrote, "We don't see things as they are, we see them as we are." We see things through our own assumptions, our prejudices, our preconceptions, and our knowledge or lack of knowledge about what we are observing. The optimist who says the glass is half full and the pessimist who says it is half empty are both telling the truth: they're just projecting different assumptions about reality.

Gary was a university professor for fifteen years. He had already jumped through all the academic and professional hoops to earn a tenured position. In our first session, Gary told me that he had negative self talk and an inability to deal with issues. He felt frustrated most of the time at home and at work. He said that he had been an anxious kid and anxiety was still an issue.

We talked about these issues in his life. When a conflict arose with his wife, he tried to communicate and state his needs. The conflicts got resolved—in his wife's favor—and that made him feel more negative about himself. When the department chair talked to him about the need for more published articles, Gary would get angry but would not communicate with his boss for fear of be perceived as someone who was trying to shirk his responsibilities.

We talked about Gary's need to be more assertive. Gary did his therapeutic homework assignment and had told his boss no on a few projects at work, but he felt bad about setting boundaries. He said he wouldn't have set them if his boss didn't expect the moon from him.

Gary said he tried to be more assertive with his wife but he never thought the conflicts were perfectly resolved. He would then blame his wife for her shortcomings. We were only making mediocre progress. Gary needed to figure out the real, underlying problem.

He came in the following week and told me his wife had said something interesting to him over the weekend. He had told her that he had finally handed in the final report for a federal grant. His wife said his perfectionism had to be in overdrive. He was surprised by her remark, and did not respond.

"Do you think perfectionism is the problem?" I asked.

"I don't know. I always pride myself on doing good work. In fact, I received my Ph.D. earlier than anyone else at my school. I got tenured earlier than anyone else in my program." He waited a couple of seconds. "But I'm probably the most anxious person in my department. I see everyone laughing over coffee, taking long lunch breaks, and everyone goes home earlier than I do."

I went to a drawer in my desk and pulled out a sheet of paper titled "Autobiography in Five Short Chapters." It is taken from Portia Nelson's book *There's a Hole in My Sidewalk* and it helps a person name his issue. I asked Gary to read it and told him that I would ask him a couple of questions.

> Chapter One: I walk down the street. There is a deep hole in the sidewalk. I fall in. I am lost… I am helpless. It wasn't my fault! It takes forever to find a way out.
>
> Chapter Two: I walk down the same street. There is a deep hole in the sidewalk. I pretend I don't see it. I fall in again.

I can't believe I am in the same place. But, it isn't my fault! It still takes a long time to get out.

Chapter Three: I walk down the same street. There is a deep hole in the sidewalk. I see it is there. I still fall in… it's a habit. My eyes are open. I know where I am. It is my fault! I get out immediately.

Chapter Four: I walk down the street. There is a deep hole in the sidewalk. I walk around it.

Chapter Five: I walk down another street.

Gary lifted his head when he was done reading. He grinned at me. "This is good."

I agreed with him. "Gary, what would you say is your hole—your issue—that you keep falling into?"

He thought about it for a minute. "Probably perfectionism. With that final grant report, I had been flogging myself for five days. I was endlessly fidgeting around the margins. I couldn't get myself to sign on the dotted line and mail it in because I didn't think it was perfect." He paused again. "I was a mess for months and months after my Masters' program. And I had to go on medication while I was getting my Ph.D. I never thought my work was good enough. It was never perfect."

Gary had just named his issue. I now could help Gary by equipping him with skills to get himself out of his hole. "What chapter do you think you're in?"

Gary looked at the sheet of paper again. "Probably Chapter Two. I don't think the hole is there. It takes forever to get out."

Since steps toward a healthier life are usually done incrementally, I asked, "What do you need to do to move yourself to Chapter Three?"

Gary looked down. He was really thinking. "I truthfully don't know. I have always lived my life this way. And my department chair expects the moon from me."

Gary was projecting and I wanted to bring his issue to its rightful place. "Do you think the real issue is you expect the moon from yourself?"

This stumped Gary. He finally said, "You could be right."

We were on a roll so I continued to push Gary therapeutically. "And when you said the conflicts with your wife are never resolved perfectly, do you think some of the shortcomings are yours because of your perfectionism?"

"Yes," Gary said sheepishly.

We dealt with the issue of projection. Now Gary needed strategies to change his thoughts that everything needs to be perfect. This would start to move him to Chapter Three of the "Autobiography in Five Short Chapters."

"Gary, there are two areas I want to talk about with regard to perfectionism. Number one, self improvement is noble, because the motivation behind it is to evolve into a better person. Perfectionism is not noble because the motivation behind it is to prove our self to other people because we feel less than. Perfectionism is not self improvement because the goal is to impress other people.

"The second thing has been told to me by others who also deal with perfectionism. They have told me that the best strategy is to tell yourself, 'this is good enough.'"

Gary winced. "I don't know….I don't want to be a slacker."

I quickly responded. "I don't worry for a second that you will ever hand in shoddy work. I don't worry for a second that you will ever not do your fair share of the workload. Using the strategy of 'this is good enough' will help you become less anxious, be happier, and get out of the hole."

The session was almost over. I reflected to two things to Gary. First, the responsibility of completing the federal grant report did not happen *to* him. It happened *for* him. The issue of perfectionism was finally brought to the light because of that report.

The second reflection was that he was in a habit of thinking a certain way: things needed to be perfect. He was now going to create a habit of thinking in a new, healthier way. I told Gary it would take a while to break a habit. So in the meantime, he would not be perfect in this new way of thinking and seeing the world. But he now had a strategy to move himself from Chapter Two, to Chapter Three, and then to Chapter Four. Then he would walk down a new road—which led toward the place where he was his own counselor.

Gary smiled. He had a roadmap on how to live a happier life (and off my couch).

Sometimes others can name our issue before we know it exists. With distance and objectivity, they can see our forest from our trees. Hopefully, we are open to listen to their feedback. Hopefully, we will ask questions so we can more fully understand their perceptions and insights. When we are not open to others' feedback, an intervention might occur. The purpose of an intervention is for others to "shine the light" on the issue in hope the person will finally claim it, so to tame it and reframe it.

"There is a pink elephant in the room," is a metaphor used in the Alcoholics Anonymous community. This is used because an elephant is huge and the color pink is absurd and very noticeable. Everyone can see the elephant except the alcoholic who is in deep denial. He will not name his or her issue of addiction.

There are many keys to owning and claiming one's issues. In the addiction world a solution is called "hitting bottom." As the term implies, this is when the pain and loss are so great that one is much more ready to look internally to name the issue and change instead of blaming others.

Another key to being able to name your issue is emotional intelligence. Just as IQ measures your intellectual ability, EQ measures your emotional maturity and competence. People with higher emotional intelligence are able to monitor their own and other people's emotions and use this information to steer their own thinking and behavior in healthy directions. This self-awareness and self regulation helps them with appropriate social skills like empathy and caring for oneself and others.

Richard, Sam, and Gary illuminate what is true for everyone; we are all attending a big, old schoolhouse we call life that is being held on earth. Each of us has lessons we want to learn and issues we want to resolve. The benevolent Universe brings people and situations into our lives so we can learn our lessons. If we do not learn the lesson, it keeps coming back to us. (Think of Bill Murray's character in *Groundhog Day*.) There are no mistakes, only lessons.

One of my favorite Far Side cartoons depicts two robots sitting on a couch in a therapist's room. They have multiple buttons all over their steel bodies. The marriage counselor says, "The problem, as I see it, is that you both are extremely adept at pushing each other's buttons."

A common statement is, "She knows how to push my buttons." That statement shows how most people want to blame others for their suffering. The truth is, if we didn't have the buttons, no one could push them. They are our issues. We need to name the issues and start healing them. People show up to show us our buttons. Bless them and change us.

Since the Universe is friendly and always wants what is best for us, we can see the circumstances as not happening *to* us, they are happening *for* us. They are happening for us so we can name our issue and heal. They are happening for us so we can build a bridge to a healthier lifestyle: a bridge that leads us to a peace beyond our understanding, a bridge that takes us away from suffering and toward acceptance, peace, and love.

You have seen from the experiences of the clients mentioned in this chapter that naming their issue helped them to become healthier, happier, and more whole, because they were no longer internally divided. There is great benefit in not dividing, denying, or excluding things. Bringing light to the dark will heal.

In 1953, Edmund Hillary became the first person to scale Mount Everest, the highest point on earth. He said, "It is not the mountain we conquer, but ourselves." This insight came after his long and perilous journey. He realized the challenge—naming the issue—was not something outside of him (the mountain). It was his attitude, thoughts, and perspective on the challenge.

The television series Star Trek declared that space is the final frontier. I think the journey naming your issue and then healing is truly the final frontier. The mission of Star Trek's Starship Enterprise was "to boldly go where no man has gone before." I say, go boldly where *you* have never gone before.

Study Questions

1) If you were on a therapist's couch, and if he or she asked you to name your issue, how would you answer?
2) Take another look at "Autobiography in Five Short Chapters" from Portia Nelson's book. What would you say is your "hole" and what "chapter" are you in?
3) Give an example of where you feel like its *Groundhog Day* in your life. What do you need to do to learn your lesson?

Chapter Two
Resolve Conflicts

There is no story without conflict. In *Star Wars*, Luke Skywalker had a conflict with himself—he had to overcome his anger and restlessness in order to become a Jedi Knight—and a conflict with his father. In *The Legend of Bagger Vance*, Matt Damon's character had a conflict with alcohol, and his inability to let go of his past and become a great golfer.

Conflict builds character. Conflict builds integrity. Conflict builds strength. Conflict builds intimacy. To make a good story—to make a good life—one must embrace and resolve conflicts. I have heard many clients state they no longer want the headaches associated with the conflicts with their spouse, child, co-worker, or boss. Remember, there is no escaping normal, conflicts are normal! Learn how to resolve the conflicts from this chapter and you will have fewer headaches and be your own counselor (which means you will spend less time on a therapist's couch.)

In my counseling office, the people in families and marriages are stuck in conflict. In fact, they have been stuck in multiple conflicts for a long period of time. At the beginning of the first family session, I ask everyone to tell me why they believe they are coming into counseling. Each person talks about a particular conflict. Since they have rarely resolved their conflicts, the conflicts are now piled on top of each other. For example, here are the typical conflicts stated in family sessions: "My son is disrespectful, doesn't do his chores, and now he swears at me." (Three conflicts). "My parents are always nagging me and I hate school." (Two conflicts). "Our daughter is dating an older guy, her grades have fallen drastically, and now I found marijuana in her room." (Three conflicts). You can only resolve one conflict at a time.

One couple I worked with were stuck in layers of conflict. The husband sat on the edge of the couch and exclaimed, "My wife is spending too much money and complains that I work too much." She interrupted: "He complains about our sex life, but he doesn't spend any time with me." (Did you know the two biggest conflicts in marriages are sex and money? Coming in at number one is money.)

Here is the interesting thing that happens in my office. Each person complains and talks about the conflict to me. The spouse or child is in the same room, sitting on the other couch, and the person doesn't speak to them. I say to the spouse or parent, "Susie is sitting right across from you, please tell her what you have to say." The reaction is classic. He pauses and I can see his brain working. He realizes that it is a brilliant idea to share the conflict with the person with whom he is experiencing the tension. Sometimes he even smiles because he realizes the folly of stating the conflict with me.

As a therapist, I will never be out of work. How can I make such a bold statement? One of the main reasons is because many (if not most) groups are stuck in some sort of conflict. They don't know how to resolve conflicts and they are afraid of them. There are two sections to this chapter: external conflicts and internal conflicts. I will start with the conflicts that occur in our external world.

External Conflicts

Since we are social beings, we are born, raised, interact, work, and play within groups. A family is a group. Friends are a group. A church committee is a group. Civic clubs, tennis leagues, AA, and a chat room are all groups. Most everyone's all-time "favorite" group is their workplace.

If conflicts are so commonplace, why are we so bad at dealing with them? Why are we a conflict-averse society? One reason is that we have been taught that conflicts are bad and are something to shy away from. Another reason is that in the past, conflicts have brought pain because we didn't know how to resolve them in a healthy way. With conflict, there is the possibility of losing something. We have missed a very important point: conflict can also bring gain, and release of unhealthy tension.

You will learn in this chapter that conflicts can be beneficial and can be used to elevate marriages, friendships, families, church groups, work products and processes. I know myself. I don't know your family, or your work group. Yes, they may be more toxic than most other groups. And, yes, you have always run to the hills when you see a conflict rising. Please trust me and keep reading. Resolving conflicts is foundational to good mental health and a happy life. Keep reading and practice the strategies. It will be worth it. You will spend less time on a therapist's couch and closer to becoming your own counselor.

Every group—and I mean every group—goes through the same stages of development. (A group is two people or 202 people.) The stages of group development are cyclical and we want the cycle to spiral upwards. There are three stages of group development. Groups can resolve conflicts, grow and rotate upwards. Or they can stay stuck in conflicts and spin around and around and around….to the point that one wants to leave the tornado.

The first stage is the Enter/Exit Stage. In this stage, members get to know each other. They talk about surface issues like the weather, hobbies, where they work, sports, their alma mater, or current events. The reason for discussing these seemingly superficial topics is so everyone can figure out whether they want to belong to this group. If there are many common interests, people are more likely to *enter* the group. On the other hand, if there are not many connections, they are more likely to politely *exit* the group by not attending the next meeting or not calling a new acquaintance to watch a sporting event or have coffee.

Some members are extraverts and find it easy to talk and enter into group activities. The introverts are more likely to sit on the sidelines, watch, and learn. This creates over and under participators which generally becomes a conflict in the next stage.

When the group is new and nearly everyone is putting forth his or her best behavior, conflicts are not dealt with directly. Requirements and rules are created in the hope that they will guide the group through the storms. Sadly, this does not work. The second stage will inevitably appear.

The second stage is called Control/Conflict. During this stage, the pecking order is created. Attention shifts to decision-making and who will influence these decisions. Group members are keenly aware of their influence potential and to what degree they will allow others to control or influence them.

This is the stage in which trust is developed. Group members quit playing "customer golf" (let the customer win to gain goodwill) and start sharing differences of opinions. This will help determine influence and the acceptability of differences. Sometimes opinions are expressed in a challenging way. Bickering and quarreling are common. Often, the leader is attacked. All of this seemingly negative activity has a purpose. It is testing the waters to see if one will be fully accepted by the group.

During this stage, members learn the acceptable level of self-disclosure, the degree to which they are accepted, and the level of acceptance of their opinions and ideas. It is very interesting that at the beginning of this stage, communication is "there and then." For example, a person might discuss the dynamics of an immediate problem by sharing how communication is a problem in all businesses. Another member might share that she has seen this problem arise in the past but not talk about the current conflict. Two friends might have an unresolved conflict, but they talk only about shopping, children, and their latest trips.

If the group evolves and grows in this stage, communications begins to change to "here and now." For example, a person in a workplace might share with a person from another department that she would appreciate direct communication from that department. Or someone will recall a conversation from the past and apply it to what he needs in the present moment. A friend might state that his feelings were hurt and he would appreciate being more fully heard during a discussion. Conflicts can only be resolved in "here and now" communication.

The main issue during this stage is each member's need to trust the other members. When this is accomplished, leadership functions are shared. All members of the group participate and use their strengths and talents based on the activity at hand. Goals might be changed because of the increase in here and now communication. Efficiency rises and members see an increase in positive results.

The best way to resolve conflicts is to tell the group or person what you need by making "I" statements. The opposite of this is "You" statements. For example, if you are late to meetings and I say, "*You* are always late for our meetings. *You* are setting us back. *You* are slowing down our process." You would probably react defensively and say, "Well, *you* are anal retentive and *you* need to mellow out." We would stay stuck in the Control/Conflict stage. We would go round and round and the meeting would probably be ineffective.

If I said, "*I* would appreciate you making it to our meeting on time, because *I* want your input and *I* want the best outcome possible." You would probably be more open to my request, and agree that you will try harder next time. At the next meeting, you show up on time. I feel you heard me and respected my request.

In my office, when the first person to state his or her problem to the spouse, parent, or child, I ask that person to end with an "I need" or "I would appreciate" statement. Then I coach the other person to only respond to that statement. The most amazing thing usually happens—they start to resolve the conflict.

Then the other person has his chance to state a conflict. Many times, but not always, he or she will address me. Again, I ask that person to talk to the family member. I coach him or her to end with an "I need" or "I would appreciate" statement. When this occurs, therapy has begun and they are in the process of learning the important life skill of resolving conflicts.

For example, Ethan in the previous chapter said to his parents, "You yell at me too much. That is why I cuss at you." The father quickly responded, "You don't do what I ask so that is why I yell." This conversation could have cycled around endlessly. I coached Ethan to make an "I" statement. He thought about it for a few seconds. "I need you to stop yelling at me." Dad quickly agreed. Then it was Dad's turn to make his "I" statement. "Ethan, I need you to follow through on what I ask of you, or communicate if you see the situation differently than I do." Ethan agreed. The parents looked at each other, smiled, and a vicious circle was broken. I reminded everyone that this would now take practice, practice, and more practice.

The third and final stage of group development is called High Functioning. When conflicts are being resolved, more information is being shared. Personal feelings and opinions are communicated in a healthy way. Members of the group are more authentic with each other. There is more acceptance of individual differences and these are used in creative ways.

Members of the group feel more secure with each other and trust levels increase dramatically. Efficiency rises because no time is wasted in trying to figure out what other members are really saying.

Conflict is no longer a dirty word. In fact, conflict can be used creatively to help the group spiral to higher levels of functioning.

Now, here's the kicker. Picture a spiral flowing upward—like an upside down top. At the beginning part of the spiral is the first stage of group development. It all starts with the Enter/Exit stage. In time, a person within a group will spiral around to a conflict. When this stage is handled well, the group will spiral up to a higher level of existence: the High Functioning stage. Since we are all perfectly human, which means we are humanly imperfect, there will be another conflict. The group is in an advantageous situation because they have already resolved a conflict and they feel confident to deal with the current conflict. They use their "I" statements, compromise, resolve the conflict and spiral up again to a higher level of existence. In time there will be another conflict. This is life. There is no escaping normal.

It takes two to tango. There are times when one of the people does not want to resolve a conflict. This person does not want to compromise, listen to the other side, or work for the greater good. Often, this kind of person is egocentric, narcissistic, or a practicing addict. These relationships are called toxic and it is best to distance yourself from them, or actually exit the relationship (or ask the other person to exit).

When a conflict isn't resolved, the group does not cycle up. The members go round and round and round on the same arc of the spiral. That is when we start to despise work or distance ourselves from another person.

Most people have good intentions, want to have healthy friendships, and do the right thing. With this said, when we are enjoying the dance with these people, inevitably we still end up in an uncomfortable tango. Why can't things always be smooth? The answer to this question is that we are all paradoxical beings.

A paradox is a statement that is seemingly contradictory, but is perhaps true. For example, I am both generous and selfish. I am both strong and weak. I am both a nice guy and a stubborn jerk. Both of these characteristics are true. We are all a combination of these seemingly opposite traits.

A paradox embraces "both-and" thinking, instead of "either-or" thinking. Either-or thinking makes us see things in a dichotomized way. We either see our friend as fun, outgoing, and humorous—or we see him as a workaholic who doesn't return our phone calls. Then we end up with unspoken conflicts. We get hurt when he doesn't initiate any lunches or social outings, or we write him off and lose the times when he could join the activity and would add levity to the evening. If we accept that he paradoxically has all of these traits, we can better deal with the side of the continuum that we don't like. We can say to ourselves, "There is Joe being Joe. You know, he's a good guy and so what if he never calls or if he cancels last minute. He's fun to be around, so give him a call."

I promise you that your parents, boss, spouse, life-partner, and children are paradoxical beings who present—to varying degrees—conflicts to you. The practice of acceptance (Chapter 4) is key and you will want to make "I" statements to them. For example, if you see your husband come home in a bad mood, you might say, "I'm sorry you had a difficult day at work. Feel free to retreat to the basement." Then you share your "I" statement: "I will need you in 20 minutes to help get the kids ready for dinner."

With these two practices, you are not fighting the fact that he is in a bad mood and needs some time to wind down, and you are getting what you need in a fair way. You have resolved a conflict before it even occurred. Great job!

I hope you are now more accepting of conflicts. With these practices, I bet you will become a little more comfortable dealing with them. This is important because "you end up with what you put up with." If you don't take a risk and communicate your needs, you will end up with an unhealthy relationship. Hopefully, you will see the need and the benefit of taking the necessary risks of communicating and resolving conflicts. You will feel better about yourself and you will feel better within your relationships. Henry Ford said, "Coming together is a beginning. Keeping together is progress. Working together is success."

> **You end up with what you put up with.**

Lao Tzu was a philosopher of ancient China and is the founder of Taoism. He wrote, "In dwelling, live close to the ground. In thinking, keep to the simple. In conflict, be fair and generous. In governing, don't try to control. In work, do what you enjoy. In family life, be completely present." These are wise words. Practice, practice, practice being fair and generous while you are resolving conflicts. Everyone will win. Everyone will grow. And fewer people will have to go to therapy.

Internal Conflicts

All of us have internal conflicts as well, because of our paradoxical nature. We all have a Jekyll and Hyde in us. Star Wars showed the Anakin Skywalker and Darth Vader sides in the same person. Gollum, in The Lord of the Rings, had an inner conflict between the innocent Hobbit (Sméagol) he once was and the immoral and devious fiend he had become.

We relate to these fictional characters because we know at a deep level that both sides are facets of humanity. They are wound together indivisibly in us. How comfortable do you feel with your own contradictions? Being comfortable with the conflicting sides of yourself allows you to resolve the conflict by more consciously choosing what you want to manifest.

I share this truth in counseling sessions with a simple example that most people can relate to. Since driving a car is a common experience, I tell clients there is a "Good-guy Pete" inside of me. When he sees another driver speeding up next to him, he slows down and lets the other car safely merge in front of him. And, I tell the clients, that there is a "Butthead Pete" also inside of me. When he sees another driver speeding up next to him, he accelerates and doesn't let the other car pull in front of him. "Butthead Pete" easily justifies this behavior by telling himself that he is busy and he doesn't need another car in front of him. In fact, he can even smile when the other driver has to put on his brakes to slow down and then merge in behind him.

Clients understand these two "people" and the behaviors they choose— because there is no escaping normal. It's a simple example and it makes a therapeutic point. It allows clients to realize that they also have two sides. Not in a schizophrenic sense, but in a paradoxical one.

It is much easier to name the healthy side of us. Clients will state, "Strong Jim," or "Healthy Lynn," or "True Pauline." It is more difficult to name the side of us that is creating suffering in one's life.

Jackie was born in 1961, and was named after Jackie Kennedy. Jackie's mom wanted her daughter to be as beautiful and elegant as the former first lady. She entered her in beauty contests, enrolled her in dance, gymnastics, and cheerleading camps from the time Jackie was five years old. Jackie was talented and beautiful, but she could never measure up to mom's standards.

As an adult, Jackie came into counseling because of depression and a string of broken relationships. Jackie told me her story of never being allowed to play with friends in the neighborhood because she always had to go to practices and lessons. She explained how her mom always pushed her and she never felt good enough.

One day Jackie came into her session and said, "People tell me I'm attractive, but I always see what is wrong with me." She paused and then added, "And, I think I attract every abusive man out there. I think I'm a pretty good person—so what is wrong with me?"

Jackie believes she is a good person, and she acknowledges that there is a side to her that attracts men who are toxic, and she is overly critical of herself. She has an internal conflict between her good side and her dark side.

I explained to Jackie the two sides of me when I drive a car. She understood and said she does that too. I then asked her: "Jackie, you have two sides with regard to how you see yourself. You told me that you are a pretty good person. And, you told me that you see only your physical flaws and you choose unhealthy dating partners. I would like you to name those two sides just like I named the two sides of me when I drive."

Jackie thought for a few seconds and said, "The good side of me is the true me." Then she looked down and thought for some time. "My mom always said I have to be as graceful and pretty as Jackie Kennedy. I always hated when she said that. I think the other side of me is the "First Lady Jackie."

"What messages does the 'First Lady Jackie' say to you?"

"Oh that's easy. You're not good enough. You're too fat. You're too clumsy. You're never gonna measure up. If anyone truly got to know you, they would not like you."

"Oh, Jackie, those are very hurtful messages. I'm glad you are bringing those messages up to the light, and I feel terrible that you have been living with those very critical thoughts."

Tears welled up in Jackie's eyes. "Thank you. I have never said those things out loud before. I believe them and I don't want to believe them."

"How could the True Jackie respond to those messages," I asked.

"Hmmm, maybe something like, 'That is not true. I am a good person. I could be in better shape, but I am not fat.'"

"Excellent, Jackie. Those messages are objectively true. True Jackie sees yourself more clearly than the First Lady Jackie. Now that you have brought both sides up to the light, and you know how each speaks to you, now you need to continue this awareness and when First Lady Jackie starts berating you, True Jackie needs to respond and talk her down. Does this make sense?"

"Absolutely," Jackie responded.

"Jackie, you are just in the habit of thinking a certain way. First Lady Jackie will pop up unconsciously. One way you know she has taken over is you will feel bad and negative about yourself. Have those feelings be the messenger to you that the First Lady is speaking. Then have True Jackie take over."

"You have told me when we have talked about other subjects that I need to practice, practice, and practice some more. I know I will need to practice this a lot."

I smiled. "Very true. You are highly motivated to de-power the thoughts from First Lady and empower the thoughts from True Jackie."

Jackie smiled. "You're right."

Jackie came back the following week and stated that her boss never gave her positive feedback which triggered First Lady Jackie to berate herself. I responded by asking her if nothing happens *to* you, and everything happen *for* you, why does your boss act this way? Jackie sat back in her chair and thought for a couple of minutes. She finally said, "He triggers First Lady Jackie, which then shows me how much power she still has. I need to learn to depower her and then lean into True Jackie. She can forgive my mom which will help me not live in the past.

"I know True Jackie knows I do a good job at work. My boss is acting that way so I don't keep looking externally for approval. If I look internally, I will be fine and not get rattled."

Jackie was on the road to resolving her internal conflict so she could spiral up and out of the control/conflict stage within herself and develop a more intimate and high functioning relationship and with her True Self.

Everyone has internal conflicts. There is a story of an old Cherokee man teaching his grandson about life. "A fight is going on inside of me," he said to the boy. "It is a terrible fight and it is between two wolves. One is evil—he is anger, greed, arrogance, guilt, envy, lies, and ego." He continued, "The other is good—he is joy, peace, love, hope, humility, serenity, empathy, truth, compassion, generosity, and faith. The same fight is going on inside you—and inside every person, too."

The grandson thought about for a few moments, and then asked his grandfather, "Which wolf will win?"

The old man simply replied, "The one you feed."

If the thoughts that create discord and arguments are not brought to light and resolved by deciding which side we will feed, it will be more difficult to resolve both internal and external conflicts. The thoughts from "First Lady Jackies," "Hurt Carols," "Abusive Toms" and "Angry Adams" will be ignited when someone is acting inappropriately in our world.

Helen Keller said, "A happy life consists not in the absence but in the mastery of hardship." An external or internal conflict may be viewed as a hardship, but it is also energizing and empowering to see these conflicts and unhealthy sides of us because then we can "master the hardship." We do that by changing our thoughts and not allowing the old, negative facets to fire back at ourselves or whoever is in front of us. We need to bring forth our healthy sides, use "I" statements, and practice resolving differences. That will make all the difference in the world for you. Your choice: my couch to work through it, or with the other characters in your current life situation. Good luck!

Study Questions

1) Name an external conflict that you are experiencing. Will you take a calculated risk and make an "I need" or "I would appreciate" statement to the other person?
2) Name an internal conflict that you are experiencing. Take some time and name the two sides of your personality that are in conflict.
3) What do you need to do to move into the High Functioning stage at home or at work?

Chapter Three
Let Go and Forgive

We are all on a journey, walking on a long and sometimes arduous road. On our road are rocks. Sometimes we twist our ankle, or stub our toe, or trip on a rock and fall down. These experiences hurt. Sometimes we don't have anyone in our life that we can talk to about these painful events. If we don't talk about it, it's as if we put that rock in our backpack and continued on the road. In time, we will come across another rock. If we don't deal with that rock and maneuver around it, we will have created another painful experience. If we don't talk about it, we put this rock in our backpack.

Soon, we get in a habit of not talking about the negative experiences in our life, and our backpack gets full of rocks. The backpack is heavy and it weighs us down. Since this is laborious, we sometimes look for ways to escape the heaviness and pain. We might excessively drink alcohol, smoke marijuana, over eat, abuse prescription drugs, watch too much television or shop excessively. We then feel better—the burdens have been eased—until the drug wears off or the obsessive experience is over. Then we are back to our difficult, heavy journey. Life might be even more difficult after a mind-altering experience, because we might have done something dumb—hurt ourselves on another rock.

People with a metaphorical backpack full of rocks are probably angry and depressed. They have not forgiven. Their coping mechanisms could be to isolate themselves or lash out at others. A dark cloud follows them wherever they go.

We need to find someone we trust and who will listen to our stories. We need to acknowledge and then accept that the rocks are in our backpack. Then we need to talk about those painful experiences so we can let go of the rocks. We need to put the rocks down and forgive. The result will be a journey that is lighter and with less emotional baggage. We might then remember another rock that is still in our backpack. We then need to find someone who we trust, and share the painful story. Again, we talk about the experience to purposefully let go of the rock and forgive. Letting go and forgiveness are synonymous.

This is a tried and true strategy. It works. People tell me their hurtful stories. I listen, we talk about their feelings, and they leave my office feeling lighter and better. The typical comment clients make after sessions when they share their rocks and put them down is, "This was our best session, Pete."

Initially I didn't fully understand the positive comments because in the session I did not use sophisticated strategies such as re-framing their problem within a theory, and I did not add any new insights to their problem.

I soon realized that one of the most important things I can do is to create the trusted environment for people to share their "rocks" for the purpose of putting them down and forgiving themselves or forgiving the person who harmed them.

I shared this with a client who was going through a painful divorce. She practiced this during the week. She came back and said, "I want to vent about my ex, but I don't want to dwell. I don't know which one I am doing."

I reflected to her that she had a great insight. I suggested to her that "venting" was talking about the "rocks" and incrementally letting go and forgiving. This process takes time and practice. "Dwelling" was talking about the rocks and not letting go and forgiving. Dwelling was putting the entire rock back in the backpack and carrying along the heavy weight week after week after week.

This client agreed and said she was consciously going to vent and not dwell. She came back the next week and told me she had figured out that she wasn't quite ready to let some of the old things go. She realized that she consciously was putting some "rocks" back in her backpack.

I complimented her again on her insight. I suggested that maybe she had to feel the anger and hurt a little longer before she was tired of the suffering and put the "rocks" down for good.

She said she was embarrassed to admit this but agreed with me. I told her that what she was experiencing was normal, and when she was sick and tired of being sick and tired, she knew how to put the "rocks" down, forgive, and move on with her life.

Forgiveness is a change of attitude. For this change to happen, each of us has to decide if we want to change our thoughts, forgive and be healed, or continue to suffer. Many people feel justified in their feelings of hurt, anger, and sadness. For example, I was working with a mom, Sheila, and her two adolescent children. Bob, the dad, left the family for a younger woman. Five years had passed and Sheila still experienced sadness, bitterness, and anger. She believed that her children were still hurt and that everyone needed to come in for counseling. In the first session, I asked the children if they had forgiven their dad. They both said yes. Sheila quickly responded that she had not forgiven him. One of the teens responded, "Mom, that's why you have so much resentment."

Resentment is the residual poison from not forgiving yourself or another. The word resent means "to feel again." We continue to feel the negative feelings from the past. We take a rock out of the backpack to complain about it, and then put it back in.

Forgiveness is about changing our relationship with our past. It is accepting the fact that the painful event occurred in order to let go of the suffering of the past into the present and future.

The two teens were no longer re-feeling the pain of five years before. They had forgiven and no longer held on to the past. They were well adjusted, doing well in school, and active on the debate team. Mom had a negative self image, chronic stomachaches, and carried around tons of anger. The teens were correct; not forgiving creates resentment which is an emotional prison. It ties you to a person or an experience that you would rather forget, but by not letting go and forgiving, you unconsciously choose to stay connected.

Sheila's ex-husband is not suffering from the experience. Only she is in a state of misery. I asked Sheila if she would like individual sessions to get beyond the pain of the divorce. She agreed and we spent weeks talking about the rocks in her backpack.

At first, Sheila talked about the rocks and felt better. But she had not actually forgiven Bob—changed her attitude—so she picked the rocks back up during the week when something reminded her of the divorce. I challenged Sheila to forgive him—not for his sake—but for her emotional and physical well being. I shared with Sheila the idea that the primary reason we forgive is for our own sake—to let go of the poison we are holding on to. I also reminded Sheila that forgiveness is not a one-time deal. It is a process that often must be repeated.

Sheila was resistant because she had the misperception that she would be weak if she forgave him. I thanked her for saying that and I told her that forgiveness occurs from a position of strength because the forgiver recognizes an injustice and labels it for what it is.

Sheila did change her thoughts and forgave her ex-husband, and then opened herself to ways of getting what she needed from other sources. She joined the Singles Ministry at her church for a social network and support group. She started laughing again, and other parents asked her to meet up for coffee after her children's speech contests.

Sheila had a couple of profound "aha" moments when she entered the process of forgiveness. First, her ex-husband had always been an adolescent emotionally. He always wanted what he wanted, without thinking of her. She had tried for years to change him, but he continued to stay distant from the children, did not help around the house, played cards with his male friends, and watched sports on the television downstairs away from the rest of the family.

Her second insight was that Bob cannot be anyone but Bob. She married him because he was handsome and the life of the party. At a deep level, she knew he was irresponsible and self-centered. Once they had children, she had tried to change him. She knew that she had made a mistake in marrying him, but did not want to take ownership of that problem. She allowed herself to become a victim.

The final insight Sheila communicated to me was she grew up with an emotionally distant dad and she felt like a victim when he wouldn't be there for her. She also felt victimized by an angry mom. Sheila knew she had "married her dad," and "became her mom." Sheila wanted my help on how to see her childhood experiences and her divorce in the framework of a friendly Universe. I suggested if Bob had not acted out and ruined their marriage, she would have never have seen me for counseling. She would still feel like a victim to her ex-husband, mom and dad. And then probably she would stay in an unhealthy marriage or look for men to date who replicate those unhealthy childhood experiences. Marrying Bob woke her up to this family dysfunction and helped her let go of the past and be free to create new, functional life.

I shared with Sheila the Four L's of forgiveness to help equip her to stay off my couch and become her own therapist. The first L is "Look at the issue." For her, the issue was she was married to an adult man who was emotionally an adolescent. The second L is "Learn the lesson." The only person we can change is our self. Bob is not going to change. So Sheila made the decision to move into the third L: "Let it go." Sheila let go of Bob and started her healing and personal growth. The fourth L is "Love yourself and the other person." Sheila was now in a better environment to love herself and love the father of her children from a distance.

When we do not forgive, we often take on the role of victim. A victim feels anger, shame, low self-esteem, and feelings of helplessness. The victim feels no sense of accountability and blames the victimizer, which keeps the victim stuck.

As adults, the roles of victim and victimizer become a mutually dependent relationship. The victimizer cannot hurt the other person if he or she doesn't allow it. In Sheila's case, she maintained the role of being victimized by her ego-centered husband. She continued to play the role of victim after he left her.

Once she forgave him, Sheila was ready to take on a new role: her true self. She was happy, involved in the community, and a great mom. At the end of our counseling, she told me she was still a little sad that her husband could never grow up. But she was also grateful that she had forgiven him, and that he had moved out and she had moved on. Sheila had let go of hatred and fear in her heart and now she lived with forgiveness and peace.

Eric was a 40-year-old client who came into my office feeling mad and hurt. He was a shop foreman at a large production plant. His employer mandated counseling sessions because he had pushed another employee at work.

Eric did not want to be in counseling and yet he had an urgent need to share. "Yes, I'm angry. Wouldn't you be if your wife had an affair?"

I sat in silence.

He kept going. "After 15 years of marriage, she screws another guy and then has the gall to tell me it meant nothing. She tells me over and over that she is sorry. I don't want to hear it!"

I listened reflectively (Chapter 8) and sincerely felt his pain with him. I asked many questions during our second session to help me understand why this happened.

Eric admitted that they had drifted apart during the last five years. He was busy at work and she was busy raising three children. Eric said that he was gone most of the hunting season because he loved to hunt deer and to fish. He also said that he was mad and distant from her because she wouldn't have sex on their "regular Saturday nights romps in bed."

I asked if his wife had any complaints. He quickly responded, "The usual—I don't help enough around the house and I don't spend enough time with the children." Eric looked down and then looked up at sheepishly. "I haven't told anyone this, but we haven't had sex in two years." He looked down, and then he showed his anger. "But she still shouldn't have screwed another guy!"

"I agree, Eric," I responded. I waited a couple of seconds. "Do you still love her?"

"I can't believe I'm going to say this too, but yeah, I still love her."

"Then, will you please consider forgiving her," I asked softly and directly.

He sat back on the couch as if I had pushed him. "Forgive her? She's the one that has done wrong. Hell no, I won't forgive her."

"Eric," I responded, "Nelson Mandela said, 'Resentment is like drinking poison and then hoping it will kill your enemy.' We do not forgive others because they deserve it. We forgive them because we need it to let go of the poison."

Eric resituated himself on the couch. I knew this made sense to him but he didn't know what to do with it.

"It's near the end of this session, Eric. I want to give you an assignment for this week which we will process during our next session. The assignment will help you to let go of the poisons so you can start the process of forgiving your wife."

Eric looked at me questioningly.

"I want you to write a letter to your wife. A letter that you will never give her. A letter that includes your feelings of anger, hurt, and resentment. Write about how you found out about her affair and how it made you feel. Tell her how it made you feel when she said, it didn't mean anything to her. Let it all out, Eric. Then I will keep challenging you to forgive her."

"Do you think you can save my marriage?"

I smiled. "I can't save anyone or anything. But if you and your wife do the practices of communicating about the conflicts (Chapter 2), and if you forgive her, I think there is a good chance of you saving your marriage."

Eric smiled and started to stand up.

"Can I share with you one more quote from another wise person?"

"Sure," he said, sitting back down on the couch.

"Mahatma Gandhi said, 'The weak can never forgive. Forgiveness is the attribute of the strong.' Eric, writing this letter takes strength. Resolving conflicts takes strength. And you have to dig deep and be strong to be able to let to and forgive. This journey is not for the feeble-hearted. I see you having the strength to save your marriage."

This 220-pound, flannel-shirt and boot-wearing, deer-killing, man's man, stood up and hugged me.

Eric's process of forgiving his wife had just begun.

Sometimes when you forgive, it creates a deeper unity between you and the other person. At other times forgiveness allows you to see the exit sign. You will then be able to leave a toxic and negative relationship. Forgiveness equals emotional healing.

If you have a spiritual belief system, you know that God has forgiven you for your errors. Because God has forgiven you, you can forgive others. Since you are human and miss the mark, you can then see others as human and realize they are doing the best they know how to. They are going to miss the mark. There is no escaping normal. The meaning of the Greek word for "sin" that is used in the New Testament is "to miss the mark."

That's all. Sinning is merely missing the mark. This awareness helps you forgive, and to love others—either from afar or up close.

We also need to forgive ourselves. It is the same process as forgiving others. Forgiveness is a change of attitude. You do not deny that you did hurtful things, or that hurtful things were done to you. You love yourself enough to admit that the feelings of resentment are holding you back and you want to forgive, let go, and move on with your life.

> Forgiveness equals emotional healing.

Forgiveness is not putting on a smile and saying, "Everything is okay." Forgiveness is not glossing over what has happened. Forgiveness is not stuffing the painful experience or denying it ever occurred. Forgiveness is a process that takes time and emotional space. It is a process that we can't control or make happen. If we honor the hurt, the pain, the betrayal, and practice letting go, at some point we will realize we have forgiven because we now have a kinder heart and more freedom in which to live in the world.

Forgiveness does not change the past, but it does change how much the past has power over us. It is changing our thoughts: shifting from an attitude of powerlessness and victimhood, to strength and freedom. Forgiveness does not change the past, but it allows us to create a better future.

Did you know that you are the writer, director, and producer of your life? It's as if your life is a story, like a movie or a book. Let's say that you are 42 years old. Statistically, you are about half way through your story (life). You can't change the storyline of the beginning of this book (life), because it has already happened. But you do have the power to start changing the storyline, or change the script of the movie for the second half.

Do you want the hero (you) to be happier, stronger, or take more risks? Do you want the plot of the story to change, and have the hero take some calculated risks? Are you tired of a dark cloud always following the hero (you) because he or she has not forgiven something from the past and is hanging on to something toxic?

A problem-saturated story isn't fun and it sure isn't interesting. If you do not change the plot, the next 42 years will be the same. How does that make you feel?

Right now, start living a preferred, alternative story (life). This will take courage. The word "courage" comes from the French word "coeur," which means heart. Tap into your heart and start directing yourself to tell a trusted friend about a "rock." Start practicing letting go and forgiving. Let your life be a new adventure. Open your heart, relax, trust, and practice your new strategies. Put that rock down and create a better ending to your story (life).

Letting go and learning to forgive is a life skill that anyone can learn. Save yourself from more insurance co-pays, and time on the therapist's couch. Your time would be better spent forgiving, being happy, and enjoying life. You deserve it.

Study Questions

1) Name a rock that is in your backpack? Who do you need to forgive?
2) Are you ready to let go of the residual poison and forgive yourself or someone?
3) Do you need to forgive someone or look for the exit sign?

Chapter Four

Accept What Is (and Be Willing to Have a Plan B)

This is a parable of a captain on a United States Navy ship. The captain sees a blip on the radar and tells his assistant to tell that unit to change course by 15 degrees to the south. The unit radios back for them to move 15 degrees to the north. The captain tells his assistant to tell them that this is a United States Navy ship and to move 15 degrees to the south. The unit radios back and tells them to move 15 degrees to the north. The captain is now piping hot and he gets on the radio and tells them who he is and commands them to move 15 degrees to the south. The other unit gets on and tells them to move 15 degrees to the north because they are a lighthouse.

Gandhi said, "We make plans and God laughs." All of us have acted like the captain who was on a direct course to hitting a lighthouse. We think we know the right course to reach our destination. Rarely is the course as direct as we envisioned. Usually the goal changes and evolves.

Many of us are not willing to change when things don't go as expected. We react, we do not accept reality (what is), and we deem the situation as "wrong," or "bad." We get frustrated when we run into hurdles, roadblocks, and dead ends. We forget the Universe is friendly and life events are happening for us. Since we are not open and accepting of what happens outside our tunnel vision, we enter our days unwilling to change and do not have a Plan B for when life happens.

A Buddhist precept is "pain is inevitable, suffering is optional." The human condition contains painful experiences like death, divorce, losing a job, children leaving home, and friendships that dissolve. Buddha called these experiences the first arrow. The "arrow" pierces our emotional body—the heart—and pain ensues. There is no escaping normal.

Buddha taught that there is a second arrow which causes suffering. Resistance is the cause of the second arrow. Resistance is opposite of acceptance. When one resists what has happened, one re-creates the experience which then causes emotional suffering. Bitterness, anxiety, anger, depression, resentment, and many other distressing emotions are examples that come from the second arrow. One will be tired, drained and worn out because it takes much energy to resist life.

Pain and suffering are gifts because they are telling us what *not* to do. They are messages telling us to think about the situation in a new way. This is easy to see with physical pain. If we didn't have nerve endings in our fingers, we would literally burn off our fingers when we touch a hot stove. We would not feel pain and not have the information needed to save our fingers. There would be no message of pain telling us to think differently about the hot stove and change our behavior.

We rarely view emotional pain and suffering the same way: as gifts. If someone hurts our feelings, we blame the other person instead of looking inside at our emotional buttons and attachments. If we accepted the emotional pain, we are more likely to see our lessons, and think in a new way about the situation. If we accept the pain, we might skip the countless arrows that follow that create suffering. Pain is the path. Accept it and see it as a gift. You will spend less time on the therapist's couch.

Distracting ourselves from pain and suffering is our modus operandi. It does bring momentary satisfaction, but in time, more arrows come our way. Billion dollar businesses try to keep us distracted from the gift of pain and suffering. Sometimes it takes the strength of Hercules not to take the easy road of distractions—television, video games, YouTube, or searching the internet—and face ourselves on the road called pain and suffering that leads to freedom.

Let's take an example from nature. A foreign object accidently gets lodged in an oyster's inner body. This is an irritant to the oyster. It is painful. Since there are not any iPads, computers, movie theaters, or shopping malls to distract the oyster from this painful irritant, it faces its pain by secreting a smooth, hard crystalline substance around the foreign object in order to protect itself.

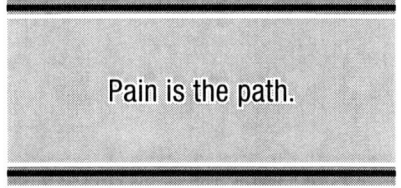

The oyster does not have a sophisticated human mind. The oyster is not capable of judging and creating stories of how bad life is, or obsessing about its pain. The oyster faces the pain head on. The pain is its path—and a beautiful pearl is created.

Rick came into my office because he had gotten laid off from work. He was mad because he had worked hard for the company for many years. He was 48 years old and afraid that he might not be able to find a similar job in a tight job market. Every afternoon he drank beer with other laid-off workers where they bitched and moaned about how bad the company had treated them. Rick had not accepted what had happened to him and was not creating a Plan B. He was starting to slip into depression.

An image I shared with him was to picture someone in a raft floating down a river. He is moving in the direction he wants to go and enjoying the day. Then the current sends him into a big boulder that is in the river. Many people, including the person I was asking Rick to picture, judge the rock and proclaim that the rock should not be there. They paddle back and allow the river to keep ramming them into the rock. They get mad and believe that the rock should not be in their way. They get hurt over and over. Sadly, they don't continue on their journey down the river.

I asked Rick if this resonated with him. He agreed and quickly asked me how to get around the rock.

I told Rick that a truth of life is you must always accept what is. For the Navy captain, the lighthouse was directly in front of him. Rick lost his job. The rock is in the river. One must first accept reality, deal with what is and be willing have a Plan B. A healthy, functional response to hitting the boulder would be, "Oh, I didn't see that rock. I need to back up and navigate around it." The Navy captain could have responded, "I'm sorry I didn't inquire at first. Since you are a lighthouse, I will change course 15 degrees north."

You don't have to like what happens to you, but you must always accept it. You don't have to like the fact that your spouse was diagnosed with cancer, but you must accept it and start the process of treatment and healing. You don't have to like the fact that someone rear ended your car, but you must accept it, get the necessary insurance forms, and fix your car. If you do not accept, you will suffer and you may end up on a therapist's couch.

A person who doesn't accept what happens gets stuck. Rick was stuck. The Navy captain was stuck. Feelings of anger, sadness, and depression are common emotional responses when one is stuck.

Remember, nothing happens *to* you, everything happens *for* you. Everything that happens is a life lesson. It happens for your growth. It happens for your awakening. It happens for you to evolve into your Better Self.

If the concept of "everything happens *for* you" feels too daunting, include God in the equation. In Paul's first epistle to the Thessalonians it states, "Give thanks in all circumstances." If you trust God, the circumstance is there for you to grow, learn your lesson, and then live in a more evolved and peaceful state. For this you can be thankful.

A good exercise for practicing acceptance is to get a clean piece of paper and draw a circle. Then write five or six things that you are currently accepting in your life inside the circle. This is your circle of acceptance. Now write something that you are currently experiencing and not accepting outside the circle. How does it feel when you concretely see that the experience is outside your circle? Sad? Mad? Exasperated? If so, you are suffering.

Now, say to yourself that this experience did not happen *to* me, it happened *for* me. What is the life lesson that this experience is showing me? Do I need to resolve a conflict? Do I need to communicate more? Do I need to lower my expectations? Draw a bigger circle that now includes that experience. How does this feel? A little scary? A little relief?

If you find yourself unable to accept something, draw a bigger circle of acceptance in your life. If you draw a bigger circle of acceptance around a health issue, for example, you will stop making it a problem and move on to your Plan B (exercising, eating better, meditating, taking medication). If you draw a bigger circle of acceptance around something as simple as a bad golf shot, you will quit carrying negativity around with you and your next golf swing will probably be better.

A slingshot works by pulling the rubber band backwards. When life is pulling or dragging you back with difficulties, learn your lesson and trust that soon you will be launched into something great. Stay focused and make sure you are aiming high.

We suffer because we resist and stay attached (Chapter 7) to what we perceive as "wrong." The amazing thing is that just because we don't like something doesn't mean there is anything wrong with it. It simply means we have a thought that makes us believe the thing is wrong.

If you lose a job, maybe you'll find a more fulfilling one. If you have a health issue, maybe you will live a longer life because of the lifestyle changes you make. If your girlfriend brakes up with you, maybe you will find a better match down the road. We don't have to suffer if we accept what is.

The following week, I asked my client Rick if he were to accept that he been laid off, what would be his Plan B. He said he would quit drinking so much beer, and start asking friends if they knew of any good job openings. I gave Rick an inquiring look. Rick smiled and said he was ready to accept and move on from being stuck. He said being stuck caused more problems in his marriage, and he was willing to do what was necessary to get another job.

Rick came back in the third week and had a hard time making eye contact with me. I reflected this to him and asked how he was feeling. He said he was embarrassed because he understood what we talked about the previous weeks but he still went to the bars and drank most afternoons.

I smiled and told him Rome wasn't built in a day. I wanted to get Rick to talk about it so I asked him, "Why do you think you are resisting looking for a new job?"

"I know this sounds like I'm a sad sack, but I still think it's wrong that we all got laid off. Corporate America is only looking out for itself. Screw them!"

"Rick, getting fired was a very painful experience. It is as if an arrow was shot in your chest. That 'arrow' was shot months ago." I leaned forward to let Rick know the importance of my next statement. "Rick, because you are resisting having gotten fired, there are more and more 'arrows' that pierce you every day. You are trying to dull the anguish and hurt by drinking."

He looked at me with a bit of anger and disbelief in his eyes. "They shot the arrows. I'm just trying to deal with it!"

"Rick, they shot the first arrow. And I know it hurt like hell. But the day you got fired is over. If you resist that, you create suffering. If you accept it, you will be able to move on, find another job, and eliminate all the arrows!"

Rick sat back in his chair. He didn't say anything for a while. Finally he said, "I see your reasoning. It pisses me off to admit that I am creating my negative situation, but I get it. I am really going to think about this and share what we talked about with my wife. I think that will help me to accept and move on."

Rick was now ready to grow into his Better Self.

We don't have total control over what happens to us in life. We do have control over how we think about it and what we do about it. Creating a Plan B and implementing it takes effort. With acceptance we don't get hit by the second, third, and fourth arrows. Acceptance is not being passive. Acceptance is not giving up. It is letting go so that you can work on something more functional and positive. With acceptance comes the freedom to move on and get back into the flow of the river—until we run into another boulder.

Ian is a bright, handsome, talented, 20-year-old college dropout. His dad left Ian and his mom for a woman nearly half his age.

After his dad left, the money for Ian's college education dried up. His dad would not send Ian extra money for college and Ian had broken off all communication with his dad.

Ian was still covered by his dad's health insurance, so he came to see me—mostly because of a big nudge by his mother. (Ian's anger and his sitting around the house were driving his mom crazy.)

In our third session, Ian told me he had broken up with his girlfriend. "Why?" I asked.

"Because she is going to sorority parties and talking with other guys."

"Flirting or talking? I asked.

"She says only talking, but that pisses me off."

"Why don't you re-enroll so you can be with her on campus again?"

"Because I don't want to be saddled with debt, and my dad should pay for it instead of taking that slut to Florida and the Bahamas."

"Ian, it is sad that your dad left you and your mom. But by resisting it and judging it to be wrong, you are only hurting yourself."

"You want me to judge it right?" He fired back at me.

"No, I don't want you to judge it right or wrong. I want to help you grieve the loss so you can accept it and move on with your life."

"I will never accept it," Ian fired back at me again.

I knew Ian needed a story to take the spotlight off his situation. (I shared this story in the Preface, but it is such a new and radical way to see life, that it is worth repeating.) "Ian, I want to tell you a story. A story about an old farmer who only had one horse and one son to help him on his farm. One day the horse escaped and all the farmer's neighbors felt sad for him. They told him they were sorry for his bad luck. The wise farmer said, 'Good luck? Bad luck? Who knows. We shall see.' A couple of days later, the horse came back with five wild mares. This time the neighbors congratulated the farmer on his good luck. His wise reply was, 'Good luck? Bad luck? Who knows. We shall see.' A week later, his son was taming one of the wild horses and got bucked off and broke his leg. Again, the neighbors expressed their sadness and thought this was very bad luck. The farmer responded the same way, 'Good luck? Bad luck? Who knows. We shall see.' Some weeks later, the army came through his small village and rounded up all the young men to go off to war. When they found the farmer's son with a broken leg, they left him behind."

Ian smiled. "That's a good story."

"Your dad leaves your mom for a younger woman." I paused. "Good? Bad?" I paused again. "The son now can't afford college so he applies for a paid internship. He loves the work, graduates from college and then secures a job." I used silence to help Ian see a bigger truth.

Ian smiled again. "Good luck? Bad luck?"

"We'll see." I could see Ian understood the story. "Ian, I want to share one more important truth. We do need to say yes or no to all life situations. But we do not need to be judgmental and say right or wrong. For example, when you're driving down the street and the light turns yellow, you need to say yes or no to that situation. For example, 'I am far enough through the intersection. Yes, I can continue on.' Or, 'I am too far back. No, I will not speed through the intersection.' If you judge the yellow light as wrong, you will get angry and agitated. When we use discernment and say yes or no, we will live in the world in a more peaceful way."

"That makes a lot of sense," Ian said. "And, it will take a lot of practice to change the habit to saying yes or no."

"Ian, there is an old saying: 'That which you resist, persists.' When you resist what happens, you are judging the situation. Then you are at the mercy of what happens. Those life events determine your unhappiness. Since you have been resisting what your dad did, the misery of that situation continues for you. Do you see yourself being miserable about this situation when you're 25? 30?"

"Of course not," Ian responded.

"What you're telling me is, at some point, you will accept your dad's decision, and move on from it. The question is how long will you suffer, stay stuck, and hang on to this judgment?"

"Since you put it that way, it seems silly to hang on at all. But it seems counter-intuitive to accept dad's behavior."

"Ian, it happened. It is what it is. You cannot change the past. You cannot edit it or forget it. Now, you don't have to agree with your dad's behaviors. But if you resist it, you will continue to suffer. You can accept it—which gives you freedom to move on." I paused. "Ian, time heals all because we get tired of suffering, and there will be a point when you surrender."

Ian was nodding his head. I continued. "We are human so we experience lots of feelings. We need to talk about the feelings (Chapter 8) and surrender them: let them go. That helps us to accept what is. We also need to talk about forgiveness. That also helps us to accept what is. I hope we will continue to talk so you can get back on the road of life and figure out your Plan B.

"I guess this makes sense. Let's meet again next week. I will really think about this and consider accepting my dad's decision…and creating a Plan B."

Ian's days on the therapist's couch were nearing an end. Ian was closer to becoming his own therapist.

Grief is a pervasive dynamic in life. Most people think of grief only with respect to death. But it occurs in many other areas of life. Rick losing his job causes him grief. Ian's dad leaving the family for another woman causes Ian grief. Ian breaking up with his girlfriend is also an occasion of grief.

Elizabeth Kubler Ross was a psychiatrist and a pioneer in researching dying, death, and the grieving process for those left behind. She wrote about the five stages of grief in her book *On Death and Dying*. Everyone does not go through these five stages in the same way or the same order. One person might jump directly to anger, while another starts with sadness and moves directly to acceptance. I am including the grieving process in this chapter because the final stage—in which one can move on with his or her life—is acceptance.

The first stage is denial, in which the person refuses to believe what has happened or what is happening. The second stage is bargaining in which the person tries to avoid grief by negotiating with another person or a higher power. The person promises a reformed lifestyle that is rarely a sustainable solution. The third stage is anger. The person begins questioning him or herself, others, and God. Typical questions are, "Why me?" "Why did God allow this to happen?" "Why did the other person do this to me?" Sadness is the fourth stage. The person understands that the death of another or the death of a situation is not going to change. Talking about the grieving process and expressing emotions can lead to the final stage of grief.

Acceptance is the fifth and final stage of the grieving process. The person is finding a way to move forward. This happens when we accept the reality and the new norm we must learn to live with. It does not mean being okay with what has happened, but it does mean learning to live again. Elizabeth Kubler Ross and John Kessler wrote, "You will not get over the loss of a loved one. You will learn to live with it. You will heal and you will rebuild yourself around the loss you have suffered. You will be whole again but you will never be the same, nor would you want to."

Why is there truth in the old saying, "Time heals everything"? Because with the passage of time, we tend to let go of the importance of a specific event and actually accept the fact that it happened. If we can know that we will accept it at some point, it would certainly make sense to practice accepting it earlier so that we don't suffer so much in the meantime.

Life is big. If you divide it into "right" and "wrong," you will live a smaller and more neurotic life. Building a fence in which to place "right" and "wrong" will create resentments, conflicts, and hours on a therapist's couch. Rumi, a 13th century Persian poet wrote, "Out beyond ideas of rightdoing and wrongdoing, there is a field. I will meet you there." Accept what is and you will find a larger field of where you can communicate, resolve conflicts, forgive, and have a more open mind for dissolving fences and creating a Plan B.

The Roman philosopher Seneca said, "The willing, Destiny guides them; the unwilling, Destiny drags them." It is your choice. Accept what happens, and life will help you (because the Universe is friendly!). If you do not accept what happens, your negative behaviors and attitudes toward your parents, spouse, or boss will drag you into therapy.

Study Questions

1) What is an example in your life where you are no longer floating down a river because you are stuck behind a boulder?
2) Draw your circle of acceptance. Now write down something that is happening in your life that is outside that circle. Now re-draw your circle to include that person/experience. How does it feel? What will you do differently?
3) If a particular experience is not happening *to* you, but it is truly happening *for* you, what is the lesson that you are supposed to learn?

Chapter Five
Parent Yourself

Parenting yourself is an interesting idea. You do it every day without realizing it. Does your parent wake you up in the morning or do you set your own alarm? Do you ask your parents if you can have ice cream, or do you make that choice yourself? We parent ourselves all day long. The therapeutic question is: how well do you parent yourself?

One aspect of parenting is passing on certain values. One way parents pass on what they value is by what they reflect (the things they say and do) directly to each of their children. This is how children develop a self-concept (the idea or perception one has of oneself). The messages our parents gave us—verbally and nonverbally—became embedded in our minds. It's as if our parents created a tape recorder or a podcast with these messages (thoughts) that run in a continuous loop in our minds. (For those who live more in the digital age, the language could be that your parents recorded unhealthy tracks on your internal CD, or they put unhealthy programs in your internal computer.)

For example, a parent may reflect to her daughter that she has to be cute, slim, wear the latest fashions, and be accepted by other cute, slim girls. The daughter will grow up thinking her identity—her self-concept—is based on being cute, slim, and fashionable. The daughter was rarely taught that it is cool to be smart, or to be kind and compassionate to others. Because it is very difficult to live up to these rigid standards, as an adult, she will probably have a "critical parent" tape in her head that drives her to live a life of dieting, buying the latest fashions, judging others, judging herself, and trying to be accepted by the in crowd.

The opposite is also true. Parents who reflect to their child that they are loved, special, kind, smart, and helpful, will have children who learn a self-concept with these states of being. They are more likely to act in intelligent ways, be loving, kind, and helpful. They are more likely to feel special. These are the "loving parent" tapes or podcasts. Those children will treat themselves and others well and with respect.

We all have many different and sometimes contradictory tapes playing simultaneously in our mind. Walt Whitman penned, "Do I contradict myself? Very well, then I contradict myself. I am large, I contain multitudes." It is as if we are embedded in a story of how our parents parented us. Did our parents teach and model to us that the Universe is friendly? Hostile? A combination of both? We are very likely to adopt their view of the Universe and then act accordingly.

Some of us are in a fixed story where we don't see options, so we look for evidence that will validate our old, hurtful stories. For example, the woman who was parented to be slim, cute and fashionable, will only buy the fashion or gossip magazines that validate this story.

The other mindset is the story where the world is your oyster, personal qualities are not fixed, and life gives us opportunities to change and evolve. For example, the same woman could see the beauty and body image messages as her mom's issue, not hers. She creates a new story—parents herself—of maintaining a healthy body while also exercising her brain and emotional intelligence.

> Every story—every way we were parented—can be changed to a better ending.

The goal is to "hear" or "see" these tapes (thoughts), and parent our self to what we deem is the healthiest for us and for others. Every story—every way we were parented—can be changed to a better ending. Write your story so you will become the hero/heroine that you were always meant to be.

Let me introduce you to three clients to further illuminate this dynamic:

Sandi, a pretty 38-year-old woman who tells me she often gets asked out on dates. In the same breath she says in a little girl's voice that she believes she will never find a husband.

Kevin, a successful businessman reports that he is afraid he is going to get fired, although he had been promoted two weeks prior and he had already received positive feedback about his performance.

Patrick, a promising high school tennis player ranked number one in his school and number two in the state, comments that he believes he isn't really that good a tennis player.

Where do these ideas and beliefs—that are clearly not based in reality—come from? They come from what these clients were taught and mirrored in childhood, which created sets of negative tapes that run in their heads.

Sandi had a mother who was extremely judgmental and a dad who was a drunk. Her mother was unhappily married, didn't trust men, and took much of her negativity out on her only daughter: never helping her with hygiene and cosmetics are two examples. Her mother would often state, "No man is going to want to marry someone with mousey brown hair like yours."

Sandi would try to look for love from her father, but he was emotionally unavailable. Sandi was lonely and had a negative self concept.

Sandi learned at a young age from her mother that she was ugly, inept, and no one would want to marry her. Her father mirrored to her that men were physically and emotionally disengaged. When she would date, she did not believe a man when he told her she was beautiful. It did not correspond to the tape in her head that told her she was ugly. She did not accept compliments about her fine cooking, or good sense of humor because the "I am incompetent and unlovable" tape was playing too loudly in her head. She parented herself like her mom and dad had parented her.

Kevin had a very strict father who believed in the power of the stick. From Kevin's perspective, his dad never gave positive reinforcement and only communicated when a child did something wrong. Kevin worked hard all of his childhood trying to please his father. But as far as Kevin knew, his dad was incapable of showing love or sharing anything positive.

The message Kevin had learned was a powerful one that played routinely in his head and informed him that he was never good enough, was a failure, and was an imposter in his successful career. He couldn't hear any of the positive messages his wife would reflect to him because he didn't know how to re-program the tapes in his head. He didn't know how to change his thoughts. He continued to parent himself like his father had parented him.

Patrick had a tennis coach who nitpicked. The coach saw huge potential in Patrick and took a special interest in him, but he thought the way to motivate someone was to highlight the shortcomings.

Patrick's parents were not tennis players, so he didn't believe the positive comments from them. He looked up to the tennis coach and drank the Kool-Aid of negativity.

How do we deal with these negative tapes or podcasts and parent ourselves better? First, it is important to recognize and name the tapes that are playing in our heads. This is important because it is difficult to discern a specific tape within the thousands of thoughts we have in a day. By naming the tape and bringing it into the light, it gives us something concrete to work with. When you bring something into the light, it loses power. When a young child is afraid there is a boogie man in the closet, the parent turns on the light. The thought of the boogie man is de-powered and the child feels safe again. (This metaphor is also in Chapter 1. It is important to understand this concept, so it is purposefully stated again.)

Sandi named her tape, "hurt child." Kevin named his tape "critical parent." Patrick named his tape, "negative coach." It is beneficial to you to take time to figure out what old tape is playing in your head because that tape is how you are parenting yourself.

Did Sandi, Kevin, and Patrick, (and you) come in the world with these tapes playing in their heads? Were they born with these self-concepts? Absolutely not. We do not come into the world with a self-concept. As I said before, self concept is a learned phenomenon. We learn our self concepts from the messages we get from our parents and siblings, and from the culture in which we live.

Everyone has learned from a combination of negative and positive self-concept tapes. No parent is perfect and every parent is trying his or her best. I had a 50-year-old client, Steven, who was a well-adjusted, successful college professor, and great husband and father. He heard a talk I gave on meditation, and he tried the strategies but couldn't quiet his mind. Steve made an appointment to see me and I quickly learned that he had a father who was a very successful businessman who taught Steve that he should never be idle. His self-concept was based on his accomplishments. These messages were not malicious, but Steve's dad had grown up during the depression and had created these tapes for himself to survive.

Steve said his schedule at the university was very loose. He had set office and teaching hours, but he could structure the rest of his time as he saw fit. He had an old, nagging parental tape in his head that stated, "If you are not at work by 8:00 in the morning, you are lazy and doing something wrong." He felt uneasy and even anxious when he was still at home at 8:00 in the morning. Steve taught night classes, and he had no need to be at work that early. But the work ethic tape that he learned from his dad kept playing and playing.

To sit in meditation and "do nothing" was anathema to what Steve had learned as a child. Steve had lived fifty years buying into the unconscious "businessman" tape that his dad mirrored and taught him. He started the process of parenting himself better by creating a new tape that would lead to a more balanced life style. He named this "balanced self." He now had the power and a strategy to parent himself in a healthier way.

You cannot change the past. With awareness, in the present moment, you can lessen the grip by de-powering the tapes you learned, and creating healthier tapes—creating new thoughts. You learned the old tapes from your parents and others who surrounded you growing up. Now you have to parent yourself. You are now an adult and no one else is going to parent you to a healthier way of thinking.

Being responsible is one value that most parents try to teach their children. Sometimes parents are too strict when they try to instill this value. Other parents are not responsible themselves, but still tell their children to be responsible. For these reasons, and many others, many adults fight being responsible in parts of their lives.

A great strategy to help you parent yourself to be more responsible is to break apart the word. Responsible has the two ideas "response" and "able" in it. All of us are *able* to *respond* to any life circumstance. When I share this in my office, most people say, "I like this. It has a lighter feel to it. I can do this."

Sandi, who had the hurt child tape playing in her head, became a loving parent to herself. When that old tape kicked in, she would talk to that hurt child, tell her that she was loved, and that she would always protect her. By being aware of the hurt child tape and re-parenting herself, that old tape lost most of its power and Sandi entered into a healthy long-term relationship.

During our weekly counseling sessions, Kevin would catch me up on his week. He would actually smile when he told me when the critical parent tape kicked in. I asked him why he smiled, and he said because he now sees how silly it is and he lets go of it sooner rather than later. He had the power to parent himself in a healthier way.

Patrick named his new tape "positive coach." He told me he could tell when the negative coach tape started playing during a tennis match because he would start berating himself and hitting his racket against the fence. Patrick would stop the behaviors and ask the positive coach inside of him what to do next. The positive coach would tell him to learn from the mistake, tell him that he is an excellent tennis player and then focus and win the next point. Patrick parented himself.

Patrick's parents thought I was a magician because their son was a happier person on and off the court. I smiled and told them that Patrick was the magician because he was creating "goodness" out of a "bad" situation. By changing his thoughts, he was transforming the situation.

Caitlyn is a 45-year-old woman who was raised in a home and in a religion that interpreted suffering as the path to heaven. This made suffering sacred and holy and a constant guidepost at home. Caitlyn's dad had been emotionally and physically abusive to everyone in the family. He left when Caitlyn was twelve which solidified how suffering is a constant in life.

Caitlyn was the eldest daughter and was taught at a young age that she was to help mom fend off abusive dad, and help raise the younger children. I asked Caitlyn what were some of the stronger messages she learned about suffering. Caitlyn quickly responded, "My Mom would often say, 'Suffer the little children, to come unto me.'"

"What did she mean by that?" I asked.

"That Jesus really pays attention to the suffering of children," Caitlyn said.

"I'm sorry Caitlyn, I still don't understand how that verse affects you," I said.

"I heard that I need to take on other people's suffering so Jesus will hear me," Caitlyn said. "I gravitate toward people with problems because

I think I should help them…I can help them…or save them. Weirdly, I think that is my calling. But I always end up getting hurt."

"You can't save them," I reflected.

"I'm not doing a good enough job. I need to work harder and better so they don't have to suffer so much."

"Caitlyn, you are suffering because of those efforts."

"Yes."

"That doesn't bother you?" I asked.

This stumped her. No one had ever put Caitlyn first and tried to protect her. "Caitlyn," I continued, "I'm a psychotherapist, and I can't change anyone! What you've been taught is setting you up for failure."

"'Many are the inflictions of the righteous,'" she quoted.

"Where did you hear that?" I asked.

"From church. From mom. I think it's from Proverbs or Psalms."

"Doesn't that verse include something like 'and the Lord shall deliver us out?'"

"I don't know. I'm telling you what I was taught," Caitlyn said a little defensively.

"Yes. In fact, you are telling me how you were parented—from your parents and from your church."

"That's an interesting way of saying it. How could I have been parented by my church?"

"The messages you heard from others in power: parents, grandparents, older siblings, church, or organizations like the Girl Scouts, create tapes in your head. Unconsciously, you have a tape that other people are more important than you," I said. "You have the tape—the belief—that it is holy to suffer, and that if you take on others' suffering, that will somehow help them out of their suffering."

"True. As a therapist, isn't that what you do?" she asked me.

"No, Caitlyn. I try to create an environment where change can occur. But I don't try to change anyone—because I can't! Also, if I took on the suffering of all my clients, don't you think I would have burned out by now?"

"Saying it that way makes sense—for you," Caitlyn said.

Caitlyn's parents had parented her with messages that were harmful to her. The family's interpretation of the church's messages—their parenting—were harmful to her. Caitlyn and I spent months de-powering two powerful podcasts that were downloaded and imprinted in her mind by these two "parental" groups.

Caitlyn learned to parent herself better by keeping an open heart *and* setting boundaries with others. Caitlyn replaced the suffering tape by seeing the difference between pain and suffering, and being open to creating moments of peace and contentment for herself.

Here is another "parenting" strategy that will help keep you off the therapist's couch and be your own therapist: Whatever follows the words, "I am," will come looking for you. For example, if you say to yourself, "I am bad at math," what will come looking for you? Problems with doing your math assignment, not studying hard enough, and poorer performances on math exams. In contrast, if you say to yourself, "I am good with people." What will come looking for you? Smiling when you see someone, successful personal interactions, and more friendships.

Mark was a 50-year-old client who stated his issue by making an "I am" statement in our first session. He said, "I am an emotional eater." I asked him what he did after he said that to himself. He said, "I go to the neighborhood grocery store and buy a bag of chocolate candy and I eat the entire bag in an evening."

I taught Mark the power of "I am" statements and asked him to come up with a new one. He thought for a moment and said, "I am strong. I am healthy." I complimented him and asked him to state those to himself during the week.

The first words out of Mark's mouth during the next session were, "Pete, my new 'I am' statements work. I didn't go to the store once to buy my favorite chocolate candy!"

Mark's emotional eating ebbed and flowed from that week. But he had started a new practice—a new way to parent himself—which would create less time on my couch.

I saw Dwayne in counseling for about six months. Dwayne was raised by an angry, alcoholic dad, and a submissive mom. He was 36, underemployed and unable to commit to a relationship. We worked through many issues and Dwayne got a better job and started dating a very emotionally healthy woman. I didn't see him for about two years, and he called for an appointment.

"I fight with my fiancé, I'm working a couple of part-time jobs, and I'm angry most of the time, "Dwayne said.

I reviewed with Dwayne and power of "I am" statements, and I asked him to give me three. He said, "I am lost." "I am not happy with what I've become." And, "I am an amazing piece of potential." I asked him to create a new "I am" statement that would help him live to his potential. Next week Dwayne smiled and said he heard a statement on a TV show that deeply spoke to him. He said, "I know my new 'I am' statement. I am bigger than my problems."

I asked him how that statement made him feel. Dwayne answered: "Hopeful. And I feel empowered to practice doing the behaviors that will solve my problems."

I smiled. With practice, Dwayne would soon be off my couch and his own therapist.

Sandi's "I am" statement was, "I am not worthy of love from another. What came looking for her? An unsuccessful dating life and a life of limited love. Kevin's "I am" statement was, "I am an imposter and failure is always right around the corner." What came looking for him? Fear, insecurity, and great anxiety. Patrick's "I am" statement was, "I am not that good of a tennis player." What came looking for him? A tennis game where he played significantly below his ability.

Become more aware of an area in your life in which you are going to parent yourself in a healthier way. Become more aware of the "I am" statements that you say to yourself. You now know there are some core tapes that are playing in your head. Name the tapes. Name the "I am" statements. As a non-attached observer, actually listen to the tapes and "I am" messages. Maybe even realize how humorous those tapes are. This will make you more conscious of them, which will loosen their power. Name the new tape that you would like to guide you during the day. Create the new "I am" statement so beneficial things will come looking for you. This is the process of taking responsibility and parenting yourself. Incrementally, the old tapes will lose power and your new tapes will guide you—parent you—to a happier life.

People will show up in your life and say things that can trigger the old tapes or podcasts. Do not blame them. They are showing up *for* you—to show you the old tape still has some power. Bless them for that and change yourself. Parent yourself and make a new tape that says "I am competent." "I am a loving person." You would not have created a stronger, new functional tape without that other person showing up in your life.

Our goal is to be awake and aware of our thoughts—the tapes that play in our head. Becoming more conscious, letting go of the old negative tapes, and parenting yourself by creating new tapes, will make you happier and more content. The result will be you hanging out more on the lounge chair in your back yard or swimming pool—not on the therapist's couch.

Study Questions

1) What is an example of how you could parent yourself better?
2) What is an unhealthy tape (unhealthy track on your internal CD) that you learned in childhood that you now want to de-power? What is the new message that you will program on that tape?
3) Name an area in your life where you could be more responsible—able to respond in a more functional way.

Chapter Six

Get Outside Yourself

Pastor Rick Warren's opening line in *The Purpose Driven Life* is, "It's not about you." He writes that personal fulfillment, happiness, and meaning can only be found in understanding and doing what God placed you on earth to do...not by only being concerned about how you are experiencing the world.

We all get stuck in asking questions about ourselves. Why did that person do that to me? How does this affect me? Why does this person keep bugging me? If these are our only types of questions, then we are destined to fall short, live a small life, try to find diversions to make us happy, and maybe end up on a therapist's couch.

It is easier to be less egocentric when we realize that nothing is personal. The second agreement in the book *The Four Agreements,* by Don Miguel Ruiz, is "Don't Take Anything Personally." If you do, "the poison goes through you, and you are trapped in the dream of hell." For example, if someone doesn't greet you warmly, he did not do that to personally show you he is disapproving of you. He reacted this way for a multitude of reasons: problems with a family member, a health issue, or he received a speeding ticket that morning. If someone tells you she doesn't like your new shoes, that statement is only about that person's opinion. It is not personal to you. It is not about you.

People who are loving—who get outside themselves—and do altruistic behaviors are happier, more content, and feel a greater sense of purpose in their lives. They are spending more time in fun family activities, reading good books, helping others, and having fun with friends—and less time worrying, being sad, lonely, or angry. My purpose is to teach you to be your own counselor and keep you off the therapist's couch. Research shows that believing in a Higher Being (something greater than you) and worshiping helps people to be less neurotic. Faith keeps us going when times are difficult. Faith can lift up our joy and increase our resiliency.

In this book, I have quoted scripture from the Christian faith. My purpose is not to proselytize or convert. I do have strong spiritual beliefs and one of them is there is only one God. Native Americans call God the Great Spirit, Muslims call God Allah. The Alcoholics Anonymous community believes it is important to believe in a Higher Being. George Lucas wrote about The Force in Star Wars. Jesus said, "…God said to him, 'I am the God of Abraham, the God of Isaac, and the God of Jacob.'" The Divine has the same interest for everyone. And love emanates from God.

One of the teachers of the law asked Jesus: "Of all the commandments, which is the most important?" Jesus answered the most important one is "love the Lord your God with all your heart, with all your soul, with all your mind, and with all your strength. The second is this: "Love your neighbor as yourself.' There is no greater commandment than these." (Both of these commandments get you outside of yourself.)

The teacher of the law responded by showing he understood. Jesus saw this and said to him, "You are not far from the Kingdom of God."

Therapist's couch vs. the Kingdom of God? Hmmmm…

What keeps us from love, the Kingdom of God, and getting outside of our self? Ego. These three little letters could stand for edging God out. Ego is a mindset—a way of thinking—where taking care of self is the only thing that matters.

An ego-driven life is like being on the Titanic. It was touted as the best ocean liner ever built. People were proud to take a voyage on it. The expression "rearranging the deck chairs on the Titanic" means taking superficial action during a disaster. This expression is an illustration of futility because the Titanic sank—and and you will sink into unhappiness if you keep thinking in an egocentric way.

People in the 1500s thought that the sun revolved around the earth. Copernicus, a Renaissance mathematician and astronomer, figured out that the earth is not the center of the universe and that the earth revolves around the sun. This contradicted common thought and was rejected by most people in positions of power.

Today, many people believe the ego is the center of their universe. It is almost heretical to posit that love is the center of your being. Your ego will challenge and try to contradict this truth. Your ego thoughts will come up with many examples of why you should live in fear and not trust and love others.

Your angry and hostile thoughts create the belief that the Universe is a hostile place. You don't want to see and own your hostility and negative traits so you project them onto others. You will tend to be more extreme in your thinking and see people different than you as enemies. This then justifies your anger and the negative cycle of hostility continues. Your suffering continues.

When your thoughts move to love—loving God, yourself, Mother Nature, and your neighbors—you will create freedom and emotional health. Loving God, loving your neighbor, and taking care of nature by definition will get you outside of your ego. The recipe for unhappiness is to be egocentric and to get stuck on yourself. The recipe for happiness is to get outside of yourself.

If love is so important, we need a working definition of the word. The English word "love" is used too broadly. We say we *love* the new car, we *love* the New York Yankees, we *love* our spouse, and we *love* God. These "loves" are not equals and all of them will not help us stay off the therapist's couch and become our own therapists.

The Ancient Greek language has four different and unique words for love. C.S. Lewis wrote of this in his book, *The Four Loves*. One of them is "eros," which means longing and desire. In Greek mythology, Eros was the god of sexual love. "Erotic" comes from this Greek word. This is wonderful and important in committed relationships, but it can also be possessive, selfish, and cause great suffering.

Another Greek word for love is "philia," which is the love that one has for a friend, brother, or sister. It is based on good times and shared experiences. It is a reciprocal form of love. The norm is, "I will love you if you love me." When we have philia love we have placed that person in a special place. Whenever we place someone on a pedestal, he or she will inevitably fall off. Our expectations and perceptions will differ and problems will occur. We have all experienced a broken friendship because of jealousy, harsh words, or distance and time. This is not the kind of love that Jesus was referring to.

A third kind of love in Ancient Greek is "storge,' which Lewis translates as "affection," and which describes certain kinds of familial love and the love we have for beloved pets. It is a warm and comfortable kind of love.

The last word the Greeks had for love is "agape." It is a love that is given freely and expects nothing in return. Agape love will always last because it expects nothing and comes with no conditions. Agape love is based upon the commitment to a decision, to consciously and actively work for someone's well-being. This type of love comes from our core—our being—and then naturally moves outward to compassionate behavior. The parable of the Good Samaritan is a great example. A traveler had been beaten, robbed and left half dead on the side of the road. A priest and a Levite walked by, pretending not to notice the man. When the Samaritan walked by, he took pity on the man. He bandaged his wounds, put him on his donkey, brought him to an inn, and took care of him. Jesus told this parable in response to a question about if one is to love one's neighbor, who is one's neighbor?

The parable of the prodigal son is another great example of agape love from the father and an ego perspective from the older brother. A father gives his younger son his inheritance while the father is still alive. The son leaves home and over a period of time squanders the money. The son repents and goes home. His father welcomes him with open arms and orders a fattened calf for a feast and a celebration. The older brother does not think this is fair. His ego thoughts were only concerned about himself. The father says that the older son will still have his inheritance, but that his brother was dead and is now alive. He was lost and now is found. The father was committed, no matter what, to loving and healing his child.

This parable shines light on another facet of love. Loving people is accepting them. You may still need to talk about behaviors that are causing conflicts and ask for what you need. But you are doing this while accepting the fact that the behaviors have occurred. Most importantly, you are accepting the person.

Accepting does not necessarily mean participating in the situation. But the particular behavior did occur, and if you don't accept that fact, then you are not accepting life and reality. You are then judging the situation, and remember from the Very, Very Important Preface, we truly do not know if something is "good" or "bad." We need to stay calm, communicate, and "we shall see."

A shepherd leaves his 99 sheep in order to find the one sheep that is lost. All of these parables are about doing something for the benefit of another. Love is not a Hallmark greeting card. It is not merely an emotion or an abstract concept. Love is a verb. Love is being connected to your essence and then taking compassionate action so healing, growth, and empowerment occurs—for others *and* yourself.

My favorite definition of love is: love is the heartfelt wish for others' happiness. We usually have this perspective for our life partner and children. Peace and love would abound if we generalize this to our community, nation, and world. (Remember to love yourself—have a heartfelt wish for your own happiness, too!)

Psychologist and author Erich Fromm wrote, "Love is a decision, it is a judgment, it is a promise. If love were only a feeling, there would be no basis for the promise to love each other forever. A feeling comes and it may go." M. Scott Peck defined love in *The Road Less Traveled,* "Love is the will to extend one's self for the purpose of nurturing one's own or another's spiritual growth…Love is as love does."

Some people are toxic. Many times they are members of your family. It is healthiest to love them from afar. Do not hate them. Love them more from a distance.

Love is having someone's back so he or she doesn't have to worry and then can have someone else's back. This is manifesting love. This is living love. This is creating a loving community. This is embodying all Holy Scriptures. This is the heartbeat of all Holy Scriptures.

All major religions challenge their believers to live their faith by promoting justice and loving others. Nearly everyone falls short of this challenge. A good strategy to more fully live your faith is to put the word "engaged" in front of the name of your religion. For example, be an engaged Christian. Be an engaged Jew. Be an engaged Buddhist. This will help you get outside of your ego and help others feel happier and more content.

A pastor was challenging one of his unhappy members to get involved in one of the church's ministries. The pastor suggested volunteering at a local food kitchen, or prison ministry, or visiting the elderly in the nursing homes. The pastor said, "It is not what you believe that matters. It is how you respond with your heart and actions." The member said he didn't want to get involved in any of the church's outreach programs. The pastor politely replied to him that his answer seemed to show he was an admirer of Jesus but not a follower of Jesus. The member thought about this for weeks and came back to the pastor. "I'm not finding happiness sitting in the pew. I guess I'll try one of your outreach programs."

In the spiritual realm you get what you give. In the Buddhist vernacular, this is called karma. In the Christian vernacular, Jesus said, "As you sow, so shall ye reap." As a non-engaged member, you might receive intellectual knowledge from the sermon, but the gifts of the spirit will elude you. As an engaged spiritual person, you will receive love, contentment and happiness, because you are getting outside of yourself and helping others. Buddha said, "Contentment is the greatest wealth."

Love and justice are the most essential forces in the Universe. Do not be distant from these forces. Engage with them. Get outside of yourself and be helpful, be accepting, and be loving. You will be less depressed, hurt, angry, or resentful. You will also spend less time on the therapist's couch.

Most everyone has heard I Corinthians 13:4-7 read at a wedding. It says, "Love is patient, love is kind, love is not jealous or boastful; it is not arrogant or rude. Love does not insist on its own way; it is not irritable or resentful; it does not rejoice at wrong, but rejoices in the right. Love bears all things, believes all things, hopes all things, endures all things." To move this truth from the abstract to the concrete, substitute your name whenever the word "love" or "it" appears. For example, "Pete is patient, Pete is kind; Pete is not jealous or boastful; Pete is not arrogant or rude…"

I shared this strategy at a book talk and one person in the audience stated she did not like this because "it is too convicting." I think her statement meant she liked the idea of love as an abstract idea, but she did not want to make it concrete by manifesting love by doing what is asked in that scripture. Is this strategy too convicting for you or would you like to use this for the benefit of yourself and others?

I was working with a couple whose eros love had worn off a long time before. They said that they were drifting apart. They loved their children and both shared examples of how they did a lot with their children.

I complimented them on loving their children and doing many things with them. I said that they proved the definition of love. They both gave me a perplexed look. "Love is compassionately doing things for others," I said, "and love is accepting the other person. Since you love them, you like to *be* with them and *do* a lot with them." I then asked, "How much are you *doing* for each other and accepting each other warts and all?"

They looked sheepish and were silent. I broke the silence. "Patty, tell Bob how you want to *be* with him and what you would like him to *do* for you." Patty quickly responded. "I would like you to cook a couple of meals each week. I would like you to do more of the house cleaning. I would like you to be responsible for the kids one night a month so I can have a girl's evening." She thought for a few moments. "We both can try and get a babysitter because I want to be with you at a nice restaurant."

Bob started to state his needs. I raised my hand. "Bob, you will get your turn. But first, please respond to what Patty just asked of you."

"I'm not a good cook," Bob said.

"I'm not either, but I do it for our family," Patty responded.

"Ok, I'll give it a try. And, I will start cleaning more. How about if we talk once a week so we can divvy out the chores?"

"Perfect," Patty said with a smile.

"And I would love to give you a girl's night out. I didn't know you wanted that." He smiled. "I would love to be with you on a date."

Bob went ahead and stated what he would like Patty to do. The things he said were all within the range of what is typical and their assignment was to consciously love each other and accept each other by doing things for each other.

They had other conflicts to resolve (Chapter 2). The key for mending their marriage was to do things for each other—even though their egos were trying to get them to take care of only themselves, continue their habitual way of thinking, and do the same thing over and over.

I also told them that there are many reasons that you sometimes don't want to do something for the other person. You might not find it important. You might not see the conflict from the perspective of the opposite sex. You might be tired. When this occurs, change your strategy and motivation, and do it for the marriage. If you only use the strategy of doing it for the other person, keeping a scorecard is typical. Then resentment can occur and more conflicts arise. Scorekeeping doesn't occur if you do something for the marriage. The marriage is not another person—it is an institution—that is important and you want to strengthen it.

Give love away. You will find it coming back. This is the way it works in the spiritual realm. Many people unfortunately get caught up in the material realm and the cultural "truths" of the time.

In the material realm, scarcity abounds. If you give a material item to another, you have less of that item. Culture has taught us to look out for Number 1, amass more and more for yourself. This is fuel for the ego—which is headed for an iceberg.

Looking out for Number 1 is deeply ingrained cultural point of view. It has a powerful pull on us. Awareness of this will allow us to find a new north star and take a new direction in our lives. You will find it easier to get outside yourself and love God and love your neighbor.

The ego will create a false sense of self. It could be an identity that culture rewards or it could be an identity that is negative and pessimistic. Both identities are self-defeating because they connect with the ego's constricted identity—and not with the vast spiritual nature which is love.

Emily came into my office and stated right off the bat, "I am 38 years old, and was raised in a physically and emotionally abusive home. My husband is really a pretty good man. I've got two children who are also good. I'm tired of always being negative and angry."

After many sessions of listening to her story and reflecting the pain, sorrow, and sadness, we had established a strong relationship.

In our seventh session, Emily was sharing how her boss, husband, and best friend had made her angry in the past week. I responded, "You were a victim to all these people."

Emily didn't know how to respond. She finally blurted, "I don't like that word, but I guess I was."

"Emily, you grew up in a war zone. As a five-year-old, ten-year-old and even as a sixteen-year-old, you couldn't do anything to stop the fighting. You have taken on the identity of a victim. You no longer have to do that. You can forgive your husband for forgetting to bring home spaghetti sauce. Love him anyway…*and* ask him to turn around and go to the neighborhood grocery store. You can accept your boss's idiosyncrasies.

Then either look for another job or do the project his way. Finally, you've told me your best friend has a special needs child. Love her and don't judge her for not doing as much with you as you did before her kids came."

"I'm going to have to think about these things," Emily said.

"Good. And keep looking at this role you've been playing. If you say, 'I am a victim,' then guess what? You are re-playing your childhood, which lacked sufficient love, and you will be a victim." I paused. "Remember when I shared whatever follows the statement 'I am' will come looking for you? If you think, 'I am a victim,' victimhood will come looking for you."

Emily slowly moved away from being stuck inside her old self which was her ego's perspective of victim. She incrementally quit edging God out of these situations, and then could more fully love herself and the person with whom she was interacting.

Awareness is your biggest currency. Whatever you give the most attention to, you will get more of it. Your choice: pay attention to your old negative childhood experiences which create habituated, negative ways of thinking. If you do, you will re-create those negative outcomes. Pay attention to materialism and cultural messages, and you will buy short-term pleasures, but long term suffering. Voltaire, the 18th century French enlightenment writer, wrote, "The longer we dwell on misfortunes, the greater their power to harm us."

Pay attention to loving God, being a good steward to nature, and being compassionate to others. (These are good examples of getting outside of yourself.) You will receive love back and feel good.

> Awareness is your biggest currency. Whatever you give the most attention to, you will get more of it.

Sometimes we need a reason to do something new. Let this be your permission to get outside your ego and love yourself more fully. Let this be the excuse to love anyone who crosses your path. Let this be the excuse to love God more fully.

Albert Einstein wrote, "A human being is part of the whole that we call the universe, a part limited in time and space. He experiences himself, his thoughts and emotions, as something separated from the rest—a kind of optical illusion of his consciousness. This delusion is a prison for us, restricting us to our personal desires and to affection for only the few people nearest us. Our task is to free ourselves from this prison by widening the circle of compassion to embrace all living creatures and the whole of nature in its beauty."

One of the main reasons people come into counseling is because they are not successfully accepting and dealing with their lives—their reality. They are ensnared by their egos. This is the optical illusion that Einstein is referring to. An optical illusion is misinterpreting the actual nature of something. Einstein calls the misinterpretation a delusion which creates a prison for all of us. The delusion is thinking about ourselves as separate from others, and how things affect only ourselves. These thoughts come from the ego which creates a neurotic, small world. Our sharing of love and compassion is usually done in a very limited way. Our true nature is being open to share love and compassion to all who cross our paths.

There is an intriguing story with a challenging moral that gives a picture of what heaven and hell are like. In hell, everyone is at a banquet table with wonderful, delicious food in front of them. Their forks and spoons are very long—so long that they can't turn them to their mouths and feed themselves. So the people in hell have pleasurable food in front of them, but they are starved throughout eternity.

In heaven, the people are also sitting at banquet table with delicious food. Their forks and spoons are also so long that they can't feed themselves. But the folks in heaven use their eating utensils to feed the people across from them. They actually give the food to each other. This way, everyone is nourished and has a heavenly experience.

This parable highlights a factor that is universally recognized as a route to happiness (and off the therapist's couch and becoming your own counselor); be of use to others. Help others in your child's Boy Scout or Girl Scout troop. Coach a youth sports team. Help an elderly person by doing yard work or shopping. Help shovel a neighbor's snow covered sidewalk. Volunteer at a food kitchen, after-school program for children, literacy group, or anywhere your gifts and talents will be useful to another person. This could reduce your feelings of depression, loneliness, or grief. Getting outside of yourself—feeding the person across the table—will help your psychological and emotional well being.

One doesn't learn to ride a bike by reading about it. One learns by practicing. One doesn't learn a new language by reading about it. One learns by practicing. The people in heaven practiced getting outside of themselves and helping others. By practicing kindness, they also were fed. By practicing giving, they also received. You get what you give.

Mother Teresa, who modeled this way of being, wrote, "I have found the paradox, that if you love until it hurts, there can be no more hurt, only more love." Living from your ego will likely create hellish outcomes and you will end up on a therapist's couch. Getting outside of yourself, living in a state of love, will create heavenly experiences. With awareness, it is your choice. Then you may practice, practice, practice, all the way off the therapist's couch to being your own therapist.

Study Questions

1) Give an example of an area in your life where you are probably <u>e</u>dging <u>G</u>od <u>o</u>ut.
2) Love is being connected to your essence and then doing compassionate acts. Where do you need to love more? Love is acceptance. Who do you more fully need to accept?
3) Practice creating a heavenly experience and "feed someone across the table from you.

Chapter Seven
Practice Being Non-attached

"Pain is inevitable, suffering is optional," is a Buddhist adage. (Yes, I know this was also in Chapter 4, but it is okay to repeat things when one is learning a new "language.") There are times in my life when I suffer. Everyone I know experiences suffering. There is no escaping normal. People come into counseling because they are suffering. Is suffering really optional? What causes suffering?

Buddha realized that attachment is the cause of all suffering. If this is true, then we need to study what he meant and then practice being non-attached so we can reduce our suffering, become our own counselor, and stay off the therapist's couch.

After sitting underneath the Bodhi tree, Buddha understood that we become mentally and emotionally attached to material goods, outcomes, behaviors, thoughts, feelings, other people's behaviors, and other things. These attachments create suffering in our lives.

To understand this concept of attachment (and non-attachment) we are going to start with a metaphor. Pretend you have your favorite coffee cup in front of you. Further pretend that you love that coffee cup because your spouse gave it to you, it has your favorite picture or quote on it, and you have many, many fond memories with it. In your belief system, you can't accept that anything negative would happen to this cup. You are so attached to it that if anything happened to it, you would suffer. (Remember, attachment is the cause of all suffering.) You're so attached to it, in fact, you spend most of your time cradling it in both hands. And it if shattered, what would happen? The shards would tear your hands to bloody pieces. You would suffer.

We are now going to practice changing the scenario. Keep that coffee cup in front of you, but let go of it by two or three inches. Keep your hands around the coffee cup, because you are highly interested in it. If it starts to fall off your desk or end table, you want to be near enough to be able to catch it. If you are non-attached, it is not in a laissez-faire, I-don't-care way (move your hands as far away from the cup as you can) way. It is in an I-care-about-this-coffee-cup-but-I'm-not-going-to-be-attached way. Now if the coffee mug metaphorically "shatters," what will it do to your hands? You will still feel the experience (pain is inevitable) because we are sentient beings, but you will not suffer. We mentally and emotionally attach to many things every day.

There are two types of attachment. The first aspect is craving, our desire for things to be other than what they are. You are trying to pull something to you because of your unhappiness. The other aspect is aversion, or hatred. You are not happy with something in your life and you are trying to push it away.

Buddha said that if you want to achieve freedom and not suffer, let go of your attachment to how you think the world should work and the self-defeating attachment to outcomes. Be highly interested in life, but do not be attached. Communicate your ideas, work for what you think is right, but do so in a non-attached way. The following two clients will show you these different types of attachment.

I had a client who was a 52-year-old divorced woman. While she was married, her husband gambled, was underemployed, and had lied about their finances which put them in a big financial hole. She was angry which was affecting her entire life. She had a hard time sleeping. Her two children were complaining about her always being in a foul mood. Co-workers suggested she talk to a professional.

In our first session, Mandy told me the litany of her ex's evil-doings. I asked her when the divorce occurred. She said it had been more than seven years ago.

She had been suffering for a very long time. I do not fully know how painful her experience was. But I do know that she was attached to her ex-husband's old behaviors that had created her pain and for seven years created her suffering. I listened, heard her pain, empathized, and when the time was appropriate, I pulled out my prop—a big coffee cup—and explained how attachment causes suffering.

I put the coffee cup on the arm of the couch in which she was sitting and asked her if the coffee cup was her ex-husband, where would her hands be. Mandy quickly grabbed the cup and squeezed it. I agreed. I asked her if she was pulling the "cup" to her, or pushing it away. She said she was pushing it away, and wanted to throw it against the wall!

I asked her to let go of the coffee cup by about two or three inches. She did, and I asked her how this felt. A little smile appeared on her face. She said it felt pretty good. Then she quickly added, "You want me to let go of my ex." She intuitively knew the truth of letting go and being non-attached.

I explained the pain of her experiences with her ex was inevitable. I asked her if she wanted to continue to suffer.

She answered with a little bit of defiance in her voice. "This is easier said than done. It is going to be hard to let go of him."

I agreed. And then I quickly added, "Please change the word 'hard' to 'take practice.'" I added, "If you say this is going to be hard, it's gonna be hard. Then it will be an uphill battle. If you say to yourself this is going to take practice, you will slowly, incrementally get better, because you are practicing a new way of thinking and behaving.

"We can all enter into practices. If you wanted to learn how to play tennis, you wouldn't say, 'This is going to be hard.' You would say, 'I'm going to need to practice swinging the racket.' The same is true with being not attached to your ex. If you find yourself irate at him, realize you have grabbed the cup and practice letting go of him."

Mandy was attached to her ex-husband's inappropriate old behaviors. Her example of attachment was aversion. Instead of letting go of him, she kept mentally trying to push her ex out of her life. When one pushes the "cup" away, one is as attached as trying to pull the "cup" toward oneself. (Get a coffee cup and actually do this. You will see that your fingers are attached to the cup.)

We spent many weeks working through her grief and attachment issues. Mandy was slowly, but surely, getting better. The next session, Mandy wanted to talk about another example. "I don't know if I get this attachment deal," she said to me while she sat down on the couch. "Here's the example, it was dinner time my kids were playing outside in the backyard. I stuck my head out the back door and told them nicely that it was 6:00 and it was time to come in for dinner. They yelled back, 'Be right in.' But five minutes passed and they didn't come in. I went to the back door and stated nicely and a little more firmly that it was dinner time. They yelled, 'Ok, we'll be right in.' Guess what? Another two or three minutes passed, they didn't come in, and I went outside and yelled at them. I was not pushing the cup away like I am with my ex. How is this attachment?" she asked sincerely.

I first told her that she was initially two to three inches from the coffee cup when she twice went to the back door and told her children it was time to come in for dinner. I then placed my coffee cup in front of her and asked her to show what she did the third time. She grabbed the cup. I asked her which direction she was trying to move the cup in this example with her children. Mandy responded verbally. "I wanted the kids to come inside." By hearing herself, she realized the answer. She pulled the cup to her.

"Yes," I responded. "And, whenever you become attached, what happens?"

"I suffer."

"What could you have done the third time so you wouldn't have suffered? She thought about it for quite some time. "I want them to obey me." She paused again. "I could have gone outside, looked them in their eyes, and said, 'Kids, if you don't come in now, you will lose TV for a week.'"

"What do you think they would have done?" I asked.

"They would have scampered inside."

"And you would have remained peaceful. See how suffering is optional?"

"Sounds simple, but it's not easy."

"Practice, practice, practice," I said with a smile. "Good parenting is being highly interested in your children's behaviors, caring deeply about their welfare, having them follow your instructions, and remaining two to three inches from that cup."

To give another example, Jake was a 25-year-old client who was attached by his desires and craving. Jake was a good-looking guy who had played the field for many years. He finally fell in love and got engaged. Six months later, his fiancée broke off the engagement. Jake soon became depressed and came into my office. He told me his story and how he was trying to win his ex-fiancée back. He was sending her flowers, calling, texting, posting, and e-mailing her. I asked how she was responding to this. He said she was mad and had asked him to stop hounding her. He said he would, but he was afraid the relationship would be done forever if he stopped trying to make it work. Jake was mentally and emotionally attached to the relationship and his girlfriend.

Again, I listened therapeutically to his story, we talked about his sadness, and I offered him Kleenexes when he cried. When the time was appropriate, I pulled out my prop and explained how attachment was causing his suffering. I put the coffee cup next to him and told him the cup represented his ex-fiancée. I asked where his hands were in respect to the cup. He grabbed the cup and pulled it toward his heart.

I asked him how that made him feel. He responded by saying it hurt but he had to do it. Jake put the coffee cup back on the arm of the couch. I asked him to let go of the coffee cup by about two or three inches. I asked him how this felt. He said good but scary.

I agreed. I asked him how he thought his ex-fiancé would feel if he let go of her. He said that she would probably feel pretty good. I asked if he would rather have her mad at him, or have her feel "pretty good." He smiled and said the latter.

Jake was also religious and he told me during our second session that many friends from his church were telling him to "let go and let God" take care of the situation. He smiled because he finally understood how to practice this adage. He said this strategy helped him with the "letting go" part. Now he could start trusting God and give the relationship up to Him.

I complimented Jake on this awareness, and asked him if he was going to start this practice. He, like Mandy, said he would start it but it was going to be hard. As I had with Mandy, I offered the word "practice" and told him why that is a better word to store in his mind.

Jake then told me another friend had said if you love something, let it go. If it comes back to you, it's yours. If it doesn't, then it was never meant to be. Jake told me these were mere words until he understood the non-attachment strategy. Jake then added, "Sting sings, 'If you love somebody, set them free.'" He caught his breath and added, "I'm going to set her free—let her go—and pray that she comes back."

Many weeks later, Jake and I met again and the first thing he wanted to talk about was a driving experience. "I was driving down a street at 40 miles per hour, happy as a lark, highly interested in the driving experience—my hands were two to three inches from that metaphorical cup—and another person pulled out in front of me and drove around 25 miles per hour," Jake explained. "I grabbed the cup. I really was attached to the old man's slow driving. I got mad and even tailgated him. About 30 seconds later, I thought of you and you would have told me that suffering is optional. I smiled, let go of the cup, slowed down, and was happy again."

When you are non-attached, you will see life more clearly and realize that you don't have to suffer and take things personally.

I reflected to Jake that the next person he dates will do something that will make him want to grab the cup. I reminded him that nothing happens to him, everything happens for him. His date's behavior is to show him further where his attachments are. I told him to bless her for showing him that, and change himself.

All of us have the life experiences like Jake and Mandy. The driver who pulled into your lane and is driving slower than you, does that make you angry? The other driver might be older and only feels safe driving more slowly. It might be someone who is from out of town who doesn't know how to reach his destination. These examples have nothing to do with you. It is not personal.

Your children want to play longer outside. They did not talk ahead of time to each other and say, "Let's not obey mom tonight and see how she reacts." They're being egocentric and doing what they want. It is not personal.

In both examples, stay highly involved, keenly interested, open, impartial, and non-attached—two or three inches from the metaphorical coffee cup.

You want to teach your children to obey rules and be self-reliant. You will do a better job teaching these life skills in a non-attached way.

You want to drive safely and not get into accidents. You will do this better by being highly interested in the other drivers, yet not being attached to their "negative" and "too slow" driving habits.

When we become attached to anything in life, we are like the monkey in the jungle who is so easily caught by simply chaining a banana stalk to a tree. The monkey grabs the banana stalk fiercely, trying to wrestle it away, screaming as he hears the hunters approach, bellowing as he is slain. The monkey never realized—we never realize—that to simply let go might lead to freedom.

Another way to look at non-attachment is the practice of being sovereign. Sovereign means having independence, self-governance, and autonomy. We naturally think of the word sovereign in respect to nations. The United States is a sovereign nation. Mexico is a sovereign nation. Even though these two countries are right next to each other, each is independent and autonomous. Each country communicates through ambassadors and trade agreements. We are interested in other's welfare, because if one country is healthy and growing, it positively affects the other country.

Imagine if the United States were not sovereign and we allowed all the problems of Mexico to become our problems. You can see immediately that this would be unhealthy. The same is true with each individual in which you interact. Stay sovereign. Do not allow the other person's problem to become yours. Yes, it affects you—just like a dynamic of the U.S. affects Mexico. Stay non-attached and sovereign. Communicate to the other person just like a country's ambassadors communicate with countries. Negotiate with the other person, just like the countries do with each other. And stay sovereign. Govern yourself with independent authority and autonomy.

Attachments are not necessarily preferences. We all have preferences. I prefer to sit on an aisle seat on an airplane. I prefer tennis over golf. I prefer extraverted activities over introverted ones. I practice not being attached to those thoughts—those preferences. If I have a center or window seat, I let go of the "cup" and practice being grateful that I can afford this flight. I accept my assigned seat and remain peaceful.

Another name for attachment is expectation. An Al-Anon saying is, "Expectations are pre-determined resentments." This is true because when we expect a certain result, by definition, we have "grabbed the cup" and are attached to that outcome. When we expect a person to act a certain way, we are attached to that and we will suffer.

When you are attached to a certain behavior (my husband shouldn't have another beer because things could get out of hand), you typically react when that behavior occurs. Reacting means you are participating in the situation that you don't want to occur. You might get angry and yell at your spouse. He might become defensive and you have perpetuated the suffering. Things actually are getting out of hand.

> Expectations are pre-determined resentments.

Being non-attached (I see my husband having another beer), gives you the mental and emotional space to not react but to respond. You communicate effectively and observe the interaction. The husband might continue to drink the beer, and you stay calm. You make a mental note to communicate the next day when he is away from the situation.

Studies have found there is a negative relationship between expectations and happiness. An international scientific survey of happiness was done by the University of Leicester in England. The study found that the happiest country was Denmark. The study found Danes were very happy with their lives because their expectations were relatively modest. One is rarely disappointed when expectations are low.

The study also found that countries that have better weather, food, more robust economies, are unhappier. In fact, the people from these countries were some of the most unhappy people.

The Pew Research Center surveyed 48,643 people in 44 countries. The survey sought to discern the mood of individual nations and regions of the world. People from Africa and Latin America countries were more likely to say they were having a good day. One of the surprising findings of this survey was that people from poorer countries were more likely to say the day was a good one than those from the richer nations. Expectations really do influence one's level of happiness or unhappiness.

A further note on attachment/non-attachment. There are toxic people in the world. These people are irresponsible, malicious, and generally harmful. It is important to be even more non-attached with them than with others. Instead of holding your hands two to three inches from the metaphorical coffee cup, your hands should be five or six inches away. These toxic "coffee cups" have a tendency to not just to shatter but to explode, which means one must be more emotionally detached. For example, if a person in your extended family is toxic, you may still show respect and show up for Thanksgiving dinner. But instead of staying three or four hours, you might stay for an hour or two and have an exit strategy already planned. If a person isn't too toxic, you may feel it is important to honor family. But it is also important to honor yourself. Don't be attached to their negative attitudes or behaviors. Be non-attached and stay for a shorter period of time before they have a chance to act out their problems.

Lobsters in a boiling pot of water are a good metaphor to help with this practice. If a lobster tries to climb out of the pot, the other lobsters will grab it and pull it back in the boiling water. Unhappy people like other people to be unhappy with them. Be awake and aware when other people are trying to pull you back in a boiling pot of water. Quickly and gracefully let go of them so you can stay in cool, calm waters.

There is an old joke: Did you hear about the Buddhist vacuum cleaner? It comes with no attachments. Don't take life so seriously. Find the humor in seeing yourself wanting to yell at your children when they've left dishes on the table…again. (Chapter 11 is on my webpage: www.paradoxpete.com, it is titled . "Find humor in your everyday life.") Remember, there is no escaping normal, and then make your "I" statements.

Smile at yourself for wanting to make a big deal about the slow driver in front of you. You'll live longer because you won't be putting stress on your heart. You'll live happier because you won't be sweating the small stuff. And, you'll be laughing all the way to the bank, because you won't be paying a therapist for time on the couch.

Out of the thousands of sentences a minister may say, have you ever experienced one specific sentence that hit you like a gong? I did. I went to a funeral of a friend of my parents. The minister was saying wonderful things about this deceased woman. They were all true. He then said, "She wore life loosely." Gong! The words resonated through every bone and muscle in my body. These words described her perfectly. She always had a smile on her face. She said kind words. There was a flow to her life. People felt better after being with her.

She did not necessarily have an easy life. She did not escape normal. She had a husband, kids, a family business that experienced economic upturns and downturns. She must have practiced being non-attached with her life circumstances. She was active, involved, interested, and engaged in life in a non-attached way. She wore life loosely.

Buddha said, "In the end these things matter most: How well did you love? How fully did you live? How deeply did you let go?" Great questions. Use them as guideposts to live your life with the least amount of suffering possible. You will then also wear life loosely.

Study Questions

1) In what specific areas in your life do you need to let go of the "cup?"
2) Change your perception and tell yourself that the behavior of someone who annoyed or angered you is not personal: he was acting out of his own anger and problems. How does that feel?
3) Ask yourself why you are still holding on to an old situation that is causing you to suffer. Yes, initially it was painful. Now you are in the suffering stage.

Chapter Eight
Talk to Someone

Here's a common situation in my office. Nick, an eighteen-year-old client, doesn't show up for a counseling session. Why? His mother thinks her son doesn't want to attend counseling sessions so he purposefully didn't show up. The father thinks his son is a ne'er-do-well and of course he would forget to attend—"he would forget his own head if it wasn't screwed on tight." I think he suffers from Attention Deficit Disorder and he did not use a strategy to remember the date and time of our session. The young man himself construed his absence as his mother's fault because she didn't remind him in the morning. He stated he really does want to continue counseling with me.

The mind is the chief architect of our life. Our thoughts create what we see as reality. This is because the world does not automatically make sense. We have to create our own ways of understanding the events and experiences that occur in our life. Here's the kicker: there is no reality outside our interpretations of it.

> The mind is the chief architect of our life.

The eighteen-year-old missing our appointment is simply a given fact. We create the different interpretations (thoughts) that may lead to different behaviors. His mom might want to ground him. He father might continue to belittle him. The teenager might berate his mom for not writing him a reminder note. I will keep asking about his ability to sustain attention, create structure in his life, and share strategies to help him be less impulsive.

This young man is receiving contradictory information that is frustrating to keep bottled up inside of him. He has much to talk about. He needed to talk about his mom not understanding him. He needed to talk about his dad not believing in him. He needed to talk about how frustrating it is to miss appointments, forget homework assignments, and do impulsive behaviors that get him into trouble.

Research shows that if he doesn't talk about these things—and learn healthy coping strategies—(Chapter 10) he will be at risk for dropping out of high school, abusing drugs and alcohol, depression, and getting into trouble with the law. Other people who don't talk about what is going on in their lives might be at risk for becoming depressed, angry, anxious, or physically aggressive.

Our mind comes up with 25 to 30 thoughts every thirty seconds. If we keep the thoughts and the associated feelings inside, they got lost with all the other thoughts. The feelings then become unregulated, which means we might act out the feelings inappropriately. If we speak the thought out loud, the thought moves from our mid brain, to our frontal lobe, then to our left hemisphere—which is the language part of our brain. This process decreases our other thoughts by 75%. We then have the ability to hear what we said which helps us figure out what we are really thinking about specific situations. Speaking our thoughts also allows us to affirm what we really feel inside. We then have a fighting chance to deal with the thought and our emotions will be regulated.

In my experience, women have known long before men that there is a need to talk to someone and most men still do not understand the importance of talking with someone. Women share their stories with each other about childrearing, husbands, cooking, their work inside and outside the home, and juggling their many roles. Women intuitively talk about their lives for many reasons. One of the main reasons is because it feels good to "get stuff off your chest." You feel better after you talk about the problems you have with your spouse, work, children, or anything else. Talking about your life tends to release tension and create a clearer mind to sort through problems.

Another reason women have talked about their challenges and experiences is that communication has a feedback loop. Women receive ideas and opinions about what others have done to deal with the problem. This loop also helps the person realize she is not alone in this specific problem. Others have dealt with similar issues, and by talking together, you can hear how they resolved the situation.

Carl Rogers, a famous psychologist of the 20th century, stated that there are five ways to respond to what is shared with you. They are (1) evaluative, (2) interpretative, (3) reassuring, (4) probing, and (5) reflective. Let me tell you something that happened to me more than twenty years ago. As you read each of these responses, reflect on how each response makes you feel. I will share my brutally honest responses.

I graduated with my Master's degree in Counseling Psychology in the early 1990's. I passed the college boards, passed my classes, accumulated my 3,000 practicum hours of experience, and then it was legal for me to hang out my shingle.

About four or five years later, the State of Nebraska passed a law that said mental health counselors had to pass a state certification exam. I was sure I would be grandfathered in because I was already counseling. I soon learned I was not and had to take the four hour comprehensive exam.

I was mad and worried because my wife had since stayed home to raise our two children and I was the sole provider. I am a terrible test taker---especially ones that are four hours long. What would happen to my family and me if I did not pass the state certification exam?

Here are how the five ways to respond work: An evaluative response places value judgment on the person's thoughts and feelings. The response might be something like this: "You shouldn't be mad. Being mad won't help you on the test." How does that response make you feel? For me, it is detracting from my feelings and I want to smack the person on the side of his head, and say, "But I do feel mad!"

An interpretative response identifies the feelings and the problem. The answer might be something like this: "You're mad and worried because you think you might have forgotten some of the material since you graduated." How does that response make you feel? I wanted to say "Duh. Anything else you might want to add, Einstein?"

A reassuring response attempts to soothe the person's feelings. The response might be something like this: "You'll do well on the test, Pete. You're a smart guy." How does that response make you feel? It might make me feel good in the short term, but what am I to do with my feelings of anger and worry? They are still going to be rattling around in me. The reassuring response is the most common response in our culture. Most people do not know how to handle feelings, so we try to smooth them over by being positive and reassuring.

A probing response seeks further information. The response might be something like this: "Why do you think you have problems with four hour exams?" How does that response make you feel? I would become defensive and say "Doesn't everyone become a raging lunatic when forced to take a comprehensive exam?"

A reflective response captures the underlying feelings. This validates the person, which will allow him to continue to talk about the problem. (You will see how I continued to talk about my situation when a reflective response occurred.) A reflective response was: "Wow, Pete, I have never seen you so agitated." I instantly responded, "Yeah, it's because so much rests on this test. I am the sole provider now for my family." The next reflective response was, "That is hard, having to take the exam under those circumstances." I instantly responded, "It is terribly hard. And now I have to go back and study all the stupid textbooks in all the courses I took." Another reflective response was: "That is a huge pain in the ass." Because my feelings were being heard, I continued to talk about my problem. "It really is. But I know I'll get through them." I needed one more reflective response: "You've always had a good work ethic." I instantly responded, "You're right. Thanks for listening. I had better take the dusty books off the shelf."

What happened here? Because of the reflective responses, I kept talking about the issue and I then moved myself from a problem to a solution. The reflective responses encouraged me to elaborate on the problem (get it all off my chest), express feelings (further get it all off my chest), explore solutions (release tension and create a clearer mind), and finally move to a solution and a work plan. By talking with someone, I "heard" my thoughts and feelings, which made all the difference in the world. We need to be heard, and we need to hear ourselves.

Connie Schultz wrote a humorous essay in *Parade* about what a woman wants on Valentine's Day. She wrote to the men, "I have some good news! Your best Valentine's Day gifts may cost you nothing." In her unscientific study, she found that a lot of women would like a little quiet from the men. Schultz explained by giving an example: "Your wife starts to vent about a friend's snide comment about her neck. Instead of nodding sympathetically as she rants, you come up with a 10-point plan to fix a whole part of her life which isn't broken. Then you get angry when she has the nerve not to thank you." Schultz then shares the solution for most men; "Don't do that. For one whole day—let's make it Valentine's Day—just act like a bobble head. You might even say, 'Wow. How did that make you feel?'"

This is a humorous way to teach many of us how to *be* with the other person. We don't have to *do* anything to solve their problem. The other person usually knows the solution. What they want is simply to be heard.

In my counseling office, many people come in with an urgent problem. I listen with an open heart and respond reflectively to what they share. Every so often, I give reflective responses during the entire therapeutic hour. Sometimes I feel bad because I have not pulled therapeutic strategies from my bag of tricks. For example, I have not re-framed the problem in a counseling theory. Or I have not added a therapeutic metaphor. Or I have not shared some deep insight that will help the client see her problem more clearly. I have simply reflected, reflected, and reflected.

As I shared in Chapter 3, the majority of the time, the client will leave the session saying, "Pete, that was our best session." "Wow, Pete, you are a really good counselor." Why? Because I created an environment where clients can talk about their problems and have their feelings validated. They hear themselves talk about the problems, which helps guide them toward the solution.

The water in a river that is flowing is far less likely to have impurities or be polluted than the water that is in a confined, stagnant, pooled area. Standing water is an incubator for bacteria, microbes, and germs. The water that has a natural flow is safer to be with than water that is stuck. Talking about one's life will help create a natural flow and help you not be stuck in life.

Carl Rogers wrote that any environment can be therapeutic. You don't need to lie on a couch and share your problems. If the listener reflects the underlying feelings, the other person will usually feel better and move toward solving his problem.

In these examples, the person *hears* her thoughts and then navigates through the various negative and positive thoughts and feelings toward a solution. Sometimes you don't have a trusted person with whom to share your problems. Or, your trusted friend is away on a trip and not easily accessible. Or your friend is the problem. You need to have a Plan B (Chapter 4). This is when you need to practice meditation (Chapter 9) so you can *see* thoughts. (You can also talk to a therapist.)

If you were raised in a Christian home, you probably have heard the passage from the Gospel of Matthew 18:20, "Where two or three are gathered together in my name, there I am in the midst of them." The Divine is involved when people gather together to talk about their lives and share time together. The added elements of spiritual love and discernment are beneficial and healing.

Samantha came into counseling because her boyfriend said she had an anger problem. She said that he would break up with her if she didn't get it under control.

Samantha grew up in a home where her parents never talked about issues and were quite cold to one another. She said that she was not close to her parents and was mad at them for not being more involved in her life.

I asked her for examples. Samantha said, "I remember getting mad at both mom and dad because they wouldn't help me get a prom dress, and wouldn't pick me up from friends' houses, and wouldn't help me with homework when I needed it."

"When do you get mad at your boyfriend?" I asked.

"When he doesn't listen, or he goes out with his male friends instead of me." Listing these situations got her on a roll. "And just last weekend, he wouldn't go with me to a friend's out of town wedding."

"Do you talk to anyone about these problems?" I asked her.

"I'm so mad I probably yell more than I talk," she said.

"Samantha, thinking back on what you said earlier about your parents, I think I would feel hurt if my parents didn't get involved during an important time like prom."

"I was hurt," Samantha said.

"Why did you tell me you were mad?" I asked.

"I dunno. I was mad." Samantha said.

"Samantha, anger is a secondary emotion. You were initially hurt, but you didn't know how to talk about that so you turned it into anger."

"Wow. I never thought of that," Samantha said.

"You were frustrated they didn't help you with your homework. You didn't talk about it so you became angry."

"What about with my boyfriend?" Samantha asked.

"You tell me," I gently replied. "How did you initially feel when he said he wouldn't go to the out-of-town wedding?"

"Hurt," Samantha said. She thought for a moment. "I was also sad. I wanted him to meet some of my old high school friends."

"Did you tell him you were hurt and sad?" I asked.

"No."

"Do you feel safe telling him these more vulnerable feelings?" I asked.

"I don't know. I've never done that before," Samantha said.

"We'll practice in here, Samantha. But the point is to talk about your real feelings. Your boyfriend will receive better information from you to make his decisions."

"This seems so elementary. But I was never taught this," Samantha said.

I wanted to test the waters and see if Samantha had integrated this information. "How does it make you feel you were never taught this?"

"Sad," she immediately answered.

"Yes, it is sad," I replied to Samantha. "Many people were not taught this. You are going to live a much more functional and healthy life, simply by talking about your true thoughts and feelings."

Samantha smiled and we practiced effective communication.

Dottie was another client who didn't know the benefits of talking to someone. She was a bright, loving, and hard working person. She grew up in a single parent home where mom made her into her best friend. Dottie was taught she had to make mom happy, spend lots of time with her, and help parent her little brother. Young Dottie was given the unfair job of trying to make sure everything was okay for her mom. As it would be for any eight-year-old, young Dottie was set up for failure because she couldn't resolve the adult problems in her mom's life.

As an adult, she came into counseling because she was afraid her marriage was breaking up, and she was often mad at her husband. I wanted Dottie to talk about her anger. I asked her to give me an example. She quickly responded, "It's so stupid. I ask Mike how much money we should give our fifteen-year-old daughter for a birthday present. He gave a very low number. I know he's frugal, but our daughter is saving for a laptop and I think we should help her."

I needed more information about how Dottie sees the world. "How come you didn't explain this to your husband?"

Tears welled in Dottie's eyes. She was quiet.

"Dottie, what are those tears about?" I asked her.

Tears started running down her cheeks. "I've never thought about this before, but your question put me back to being an eight-year-old and I was always afraid to tell my mom about a problem because she would yell at me. I guess I hate conflict."

I reflected back to Dottie what I had heard. "You didn't feel safe as a child to talk about the normal bumps on the road in your life or when mom expected too much from you."

"Yes," she said emphatically. "But I do feel safe with my husband. He's a really good guy. Why do I overreact with him?"

"Why do you?" I wanted Dottie to talk about it so she could connect the dots.

She smiled while she talked through her tears. "I married a strong man who easily makes decisions. I probably liked that because I had to make too many decisions as a child. But now I'm an adult—a good mom who has thoughts and ideas on how to raise our child. So I wanted someone to make the decisions, but it pisses me off when he decides differently from how I think it should be done."

"You're in a double bind. You want your husband to make the decisions. But you don't like it when he makes a decision that you don't agree with," I reflected to her.

"Yeah."

"What are you going to do about this?"

"Talk to my husband?" she asked.

"That sounds like a question," I reflected to her.

"Okay, okay, I will talk to my husband."

"Dottie, one more question. Your husband stating a low dollar amount for your daughter's birthday present—how did that not happen *to* you and actually happened *for* you?"

She thought for a moment. "That happened for me because I need to heal my childhood issues and learn to speak my truth as an adult."

"A+," I responded. "With that perspective, you can live the truth, 'bless my husband and change me.'"

Dottie has her own unique life issues to deal with. What we have in common with Dottie is the need to talk about what is going on in our lives. When we hear our self-talk, we can better figure out how to resolve the problem. The second thing we have in common with Dottie is the need to talk to other people in our lives with whom we have a conflict. The third thing is to change our perspective and see how the situation is for our healing and growth.

In couples and family counseling, most people communicate to me about another person—who is in the same room! I say politely, "please say that to your son" (or wife, etc.). They stop with a surprised look on their faces. They are not used to talking directly to a family member about issues. When they do communicate directly, there is a greater chance of the issue being resolved and the people staying off my couch.

Research on people who experience trauma shows that one of the best ways for healing is to talk about the traumatic event Retelling the story, over and over, reprocessing in a new way, will help the person release the negative, toxic feelings, and allow the body to release any held energy from the traumatic event. Simply talking—to a trusted person—will help the healing process.

An example of a traumatic event is a person who experienced sexual abuse as a child. If this person never told another person, he or she is holding a secret. This poisonous secret is affecting many areas of his or her life. Talking about this secret breaks the powerful hold it has on the person. In therapy, if a person talks about the abuse for the first time with me, a therapeutic assignment is for the client to tell another trusted person about the childhood abuse. This more fully allows the release of negative, toxic feelings, and allows harmful stored energy in the body to be released.

Feelings are energy in motion. Anger is a different energy than sadness. Frustration is a different energy than happiness. Usually we feel safe allowing the energy of happiness to fully move into laughter, smiling, and talking about a happy experience. Many times we don't allow the energy of anger, sadness, embarrassment, or frustration to move. We stuff those feelings deep inside of us. Then we become a walking time bomb or become depressed.

One of the most effective ways to move that energy—those feelings—is to talk about the experience that created those feelings. Talking about the experience releases the feelings from the place where we stuffed them.

The fast-flowing water of a river is far less likely to contain impurities than trapped water in swamps and bogs. Standing water cultivates the growth of unhealthy bacteria and can become a cesspool. Expressing thoughts and feelings lets go of emotional impurities. Blocked thoughts and feelings create a toxic existence. The pressure of the blockage can then explode in anger, or result in depression.

When clients tells me about an experience in their life, I ask them to tell me how that made them feel. The reason for this question is to help them move that toxic energy and incrementally let go of it. Talking about feelings helps us let go of the past, keeps us off the therapist's couch, and teaches us to be our own counselors.

What I do is called talk therapy. It is called that because it is therapeutic to talk! We are hard-wired for connecting to others. Take a calculated risk and talk to a safe person about what is going on in your life. If you currently don't have that person, create the opportunity for one by practicing reflective listening to the people in your life. They will talk more with you, which will build trust for mutual sharing down the road.

Study Questions

1) Practice reflective listening. Practice some more. How did the other person respond to you?
2) Practice *being* with another person. Don't *do* much. Listen. Be. Reflect. How was the experience for you? How do you think it was for the other person?
3) Take a calculated risk and talk to a safe person about something that is bothering you. How did you feel afterwards?

Chapter Nine
See Your Thoughts

By now, you have read many, many times about the power of your thoughts. You have probably tried to let go of negative thoughts and replace them with healthier, more functional ones. But the negative thoughts that come from the ego keep reappearing and still create havoc in your life. Trying to stop invasive thoughts is like trying to hold a ball under water. The ball keeps popping up in front of you. Try a new strategy. Let the ball float and quit fighting with it. See your thoughts and let them be. Watch them with deep interest. Be unafraid and see them as impersonal. Let them dissolve like clouds in the big, expansive sky. Or let them float away on the current of a river. Or picture yourself stepping behind the thoughts so you don't get attached to them. Be open and soon they will lose power and you can then choose a new, healthier thought to guide you.

The key is to not identify with the thoughts. They are merely thoughts. You are not your thoughts!

Meditation is the best way to see your thoughts and let go of them. Usually, when I suggest meditation, people tell me they're too busy and don't have time to meditate.

What if I told you that meditation lowers stress hormones in your body? You will feel less tension during your day. Meditation helps you have a clearer mind so you see things more objectively. This means you are making better decisions and creating a better life. Meditation helps you regulate your emotions so you don't overreact. This will help you at work and at home. Meditation helps you connect to your True Self so you will

become more loving and compassionate. You will sleep better. Y
a stronger immune system. You will experience higher levels c

Fourth and fifth graders' math scores went up 15% after ¡
in a mindfulness meditation program versus those who didn't participate. A Harvard study showed that mindfulness meditation increased gray matter in brain areas associated with memory, learning, and compassion.

Will you now consider practicing mediation?

There are many different ways to meditate. There are hundreds of books on meditation. Here is a brief tutorial on a method for a simple meditation that paradoxically, is quite profound. By practicing this meditation, you will quiet your mind, so you will see your thoughts and not allow them to drive you anymore.

It is important to start meditation by sitting somewhere with your back straight. You may sit in the lotus position. If you are new to the practice, you can sit in a chair or sofa with a pillow at your back to help you keep your back straight and both feet on the ground. It is beneficial to select a regular time to sit and meditate. Maybe it's in the morning after your shower. It could be at 9:00 after the kids are put to bed, although at this time you could nod off to sleep during your meditation. Establish a routine to maintain this healthy, new habit.

Start your meditation practice with two or three minutes. Add a minute a week. Or access some guided mediations and become comfortable with this type of meditation before switching to your own meditation program.

The mind can only be one place at a time. You're either thinking of this or that. Now, the "this" and "that" flick back and forth quicker than a flea, but the mind can only be one place at a time. Since we want to train our mind to be still, we must focus our mind on one positive and neutralizing thing.

While you are sitting, practice focusing on, and being aware of, each breath that comes in through and out of your nostrils. Breathe from your stomach. When you inhale, let your stomach out. When you exhale, your stomach will relax inward. In time, and with more awareness, you will start to feel the coolness in and warmth out of your nostrils. The mind must have something to occupy it. Give it only one thing—your breath.

A discursive thought will enter your mind while you are practicing being aware of your breath. For example, "Oh, I need to return the library book," or "Why hasn't Terri got back to me?" That's okay. The goal is to be an observer and watch your thoughts in an unattached way. Picture a river and the current taking the thoughts away from you. Or, have you, the observer, step behind the thought, see it as merely a thought, and let it go. Keep going back to your awareness of each breath. Breathe in and breathe out. You will soon become more present. You will experience nonjudgmental awareness. The thoughts and judgments about the past and the future will fade. You will become more whole because your thoughts won't be about your scattered experiences.

Another thought will appear. Remember, you are the observer, so you can watch the thought in an impersonal way. Do not identify with the thought. It is just a thought. Let the thought go while you re-gain awareness of your breath. This practice takes the untrained, undisciplined, everyday mind and creates the development of bare attention. This is a single-minded awareness of each and every thought. This practice is to simply observe the mind, and the feelings it creates. Have a deep interest in this process of watching your thoughts. Be unattached and impartial to each and every thought. Simply resting in an open, unafraid state creates awareness and a peace that will help you when a difficult situation occurs.

Most people believe their thoughts are beyond their control. It is true that we have many thoughts whose source or origin we do not know. But we do have power over how these random thoughts affect us and guide our lives. Through practice, your powers of observation of yourself will increase. You will see your unbidden thoughts of desires and aversions that create anxiety, anger, or depression. For example, "I can't believe I said such an idiotic thing!" Or, "Natalie can't run over me and get away with it." Or, "I have to get promoted or I will be stuck the rest of my working years." These are the thicket of thoughts in which your heart and mind get caught over and over. Do not fight and try to push these thoughts away, but continually surrender, not to avoid them but to release them. Unless you want to play the role of victim, you must let them go. The Beatles song "Let It Be" is a good anthem to help you accept the past and not have it dominate your present day experiences.

A helpful image is to see your thoughts as clouds in the sky. Thoughts can vanish just like clouds naturally disperse. Do not try to push away your thoughts. Allow them to gradually dissolve just like the clouds.

Identifying with your thoughts is like the sky thinking and identifying with the clouds: "These are my clouds. I hate them when they formulate in this particular way. They should be different. They should get out of my life." You can see the silliness of this. The same is true with the thoughts that appear in your mind. "See" the thoughts, do not be judgmental, and know they will dissipate with your meditative practices.

The peaceful and quiet mind is like the crystal blue sky. I ask clients if the sky is any other color than blue. They usually say "Yes, the sky can also be gray." I respond to them that the clouds can be gray, but above those clouds, the sky is always blue. If you are feeling gray, you are probably holding on to a dark thought. Let the thought go. Let it dissolve. Your mind will return to its true nature of peace and contentment.

Most people react to what happens to them. These knee-jerk reactions may be filled with anger, resentment, hurt, or fear. These emotions fuel the negative situation, and the conflict (Chapter 2) remains or even gets worse. Instead of reacting, we need to create some mental space and then respond to each and every situation. Responding means you see your instant, habitual, reactive thoughts, let them go, and think about what is the healthiest thing to say to the other person. A response allows you to help resolve the conflict, and not stay stuck in a negative emotional state.

Psychiatrist, author, and Holocaust survivor Viktor Frankl wrote, "Between stimulus and response there is a space. In that space, there is our power to choose our response. In our response lies our growth and our freedom." The practice of meditation will help you create the space between someone's inane action and your response. You will be more likely not to react and add fuel to the fire. You will have the freedom to respond in a healthier and more functional way.

I have discussed at length the idea of being aware of your thoughts in a non-personal way. You can maintain a non-personal position because you are not your thoughts. Thoughts are merely thoughts. They are not you! You can decide to act upon a thought, but that is merely a behavior. This is not your essence. Knowing you are not your thoughts will give you the freedom to make an even healthier choice. Remember in Chapter 3 where it was pointed out you are the writer, director, and producer of your life? You learned how to think about the world from your parents, older siblings, church, and many other places. You are not those thoughts that you learned during your childhood. Create some new, healthier thoughts that will create a new script for your life. See the old thoughts that guided you to the middle of your "book" (life). Let those thoughts go, learn new thoughts that will create healthier ways to be in the world. Have the hero (you) live a life with more meaning and purpose.

Alicia, a forty-five year-old client, had a mom who always found the negative. She nitpicked young Alicia, never told her that she loved her, and favored Alicia's older brother. Alicia came into counseling because she had marriage problems and knew she was too negative toward her husband. She wanted to save her marriage, but she was always mad about his habits of leaving his toiletries out on the bathroom counter, watching too much television, not helping with household chores, and leaving his clothes draped over chairs and couches. She said she always felt scattered and overwhelmed.

"Do you have a chronically stressed mind?" I asked Alicia.

"I never thought of it that way, but yes, it is chronically stressed," Alicia answered.

"Does that stress make you take things personally?" I asked.

"Yes," she exclaimed.

"Does that stressful mind make you over react to situations?" I asked.

"Yes," she exclaimed again.

"Do you try to control everything in your environment to try and stop all this suffering?"

Alicia thought about my question. "Yes, and it's exhausting."

I taught Alicia this simple way of meditating. In my office, I gave her a pad of paper and a pen. I had her sit for three minutes, close her eyes, and watch her thoughts. Every time she "saw" a thought, she was to make a chicken scratch on the paper. I coached her to be non-attached to the thoughts. She was to be open and highly interested in them, but impartial and unafraid. After the three minutes, I had her count the chicken scratches. She was amazed. There were 45 marks. This equates to 900 thoughts in an hour! No wonder she felt scattered and overwhelmed.

I asked Alicia if there were a pattern of thoughts that popped up more often than others. She frowned and told me there were a lot of thoughts about her husband. I asked her why she frowned. She answered that this showed how the problem will never end because she thinks too much about them. I gently replied that the opposite is true: she now had the ability to let those thoughts go. She now had the ability to not *react* in a negative way to her husband, but *respond* to the behaviors in a healthier way.

Alicia was given two assignments. The first was to continue to watch her thoughts at home. The second assignment was to see a behavior of her husband as not happening to her but for her. She was then challenged to let go of the negative thoughts that created the inner stress and marital tension and communicate her needs. She later reported that her marriage was better and she was actually having fun seeing the absurdity of some of her thoughts and then letting them go.

I had seen another client, David, in my office off and on for years. He was a high- powered executive of a national chain of restaurants. He was earning a large six-figure income, but was anxious and depressed. David had a big heart and everyone loved him. However, once he was promoted to his current position, he had to start taking anti-depressants and anti-anxiety medication.

David called me and wanted to start up counseling again. When he arrived at my office, he said, "Pete, I've been having panic attacks. I can't get out of bed in the morning. I've been miserable for months. I've been talking with the board president, and the board will allow me to resign and become a consultant to the restaurant managers in a five-state-region. It will be way less stressful and I think I will like it."

"Great, then what is the issue?" I asked.

David thought for a moment. He looked up and said "I want to be known as the boss. I don't want all the headaches and stresses, but I still want people to look at me as the boss. I want to sit with my friends at restaurants and they know I'm the executive vice president of operations."

"David…" I started.

"I know, I know. These are thoughts from my ego. But I've been feeding my ego steak for years. I don't want hamburger."

I smiled. "David, I compliment you. You are seeing your thoughts. You know they are thoughts from your ego mind. You know you have been feeding those thoughts for years and they don't want to dine from a healthier menu." I paused. "David, you are a spiritual man. What are the thoughts that come to you when you're connected to your Source?"

David's eyes sparkled. I knew he loved the question. He finally answered. "I am a loving person who strives to connect the love to others and between others."

"Can you do that better as a consultant or executive vice president?" I asked.

"Consultant," David answered immediately.

"You answered that very quickly," I reflected.

"That's because I tried to be a loving person as the boss, but I couldn't. I only became depressed and anxious. I realized anger and fear were always bubbling under the surface." He paused. "I also realized that if I quit my position, I start thinking about what my life will look like in the future. It can paralyze me with fear."

"David, the future is an illusion. It is not real. Only the present moment is real. Your thoughts make it feel real because your mind is manufacturing some future scenario, which is creating feelings that you are experiencing in the present moment. These are false stressors that you can eliminate by bringing your mind back to the present moment.

I paused so this could sink in. "Which thoughts do you want to follow? Your ego thoughts or your spiritual thoughts?"

"Spiritual, but I know the ego thoughts will keep rearing their ugly heads."

"They will. You're in a habit of thinking a certain way. Keep seeing them. Acknowledge them. Realize the truth, and then let them go. In fact, on a piece of paper at home, draw a line down the middle of the paper. Title the left side Ego Thoughts. Title the right side Spiritual Thoughts. When you catch yourself with a negative ego thought, write it down. Then spend a minute and create a spiritual thought. Write it down. This is a great strategy to see your thoughts and decide which one you want to follow."

"You make it sound like it's simple."

"Simple isn't easy. Practice, practice, practice," I said with a reassuring smile.

Another client, Jimmy, was a twenty-six-year old student at a large university. He told me over the phone he wanted to talk about his inability to graduate from college, problems with his girlfriend, and a low level of depression. We had a difficult time coming up with a time to meet because he worked full time, and he was taking three classes. When we finally found a time that worked for the both of us, Jimmy talked about his work, his major, and his girlfriend. While he was telling me about his current life situation, he twice stated that his dad did not approve of his girlfriend and that his dad had told him that he didn't think he would ever graduate from college.

I reflected to Jimmy that it must be frustrating that his dad was negative and pessimistic toward him. Jimmy agreed, but changed the subject back to himself. He talked about his inability to commit to his girlfriend and graduate from college.

I asked Jimmy if his classes were too difficult for him. He shook his head and told me when he concentrates, he gets good grades. I asked him if he loved the girl his was dating. He smiled, nodded his head, and said yes. I asked how often his dad tells him those disapproving remarks. He told me he only talks to his dad two or three times a year. I gave Jimmy a questioning look, and he told me that he picked a college six states away so he wouldn't have to interact with his family. He told me that his dad is an alcoholic, his mom enables him, and his two younger brothers are pissed off at the world.

I complimented Jimmy on escaping that toxic environment, and again reflected that I was sorry that his dad was so negative toward him. I said that the geographic distance was important, but there was a possibility that his dad was still living in Jimmy's head. I went on to explain that Jimmy's dad made up stories about how Jimmy's life would not amount to anything. Jimmy learned that story, because it was told by one of the most important people in his life. We all, to varying degrees, take on our parents' stories. I gently reflected that Jimmy might still be unconsciously living that story.

I taught Jimmy the simple mediation strategies and asked him during the next week to "see" his thoughts and "see" if that storyline was still buzzing around in his head. He agreed and the following week, he told me that the negative messages are still there. Jimmy said he had thought that it was his own outlook on life, which had confused him because he thought of himself as a generally positive guy. He now had the insight that the negative thoughts were the old messages that his dad gave him all during his childhood and adolescence.

I challenged Jimmy to continue meditating, and to not identify with those negative thoughts. He needed to see them, acknowledge them, and let the "clouds" dissipate. I then asked Jimmy what new story he wanted to create for his life. He smiled and told me he sees himself in a superman's cape, and he will accomplish his goal of finishing the final class work. He said he wants to create the story of having a happy, healthy relationship with his girlfriend. He decided to share this with her on their date this weekend.

Healing takes place when we shine the light and bring awareness to the painful areas of our life. Seeing these thoughts will help de-power the internal critical parent, and give us the mental space to create healthier thoughts, and take action in a positive, functional way.

The study of your own mind is the most important "class" you will ever take. Initially, the homework—the practice of meditation—is frustrating. Distracting thoughts are the natural movement of the mind. With practice, the chattering mind will slow down. The mind will soften. The space of awareness will become larger and larger. Then, we will be able to access an Intelligence that isn't led by an ego mind that is reactive.

With a close examination of your everyday mind, you will live more in a state of mindfulness and awareness of what is really happening in your life—right now! This is one of the greatest benefits that comes from meditation: living in the present moment. Our mind can take us to the past and re-live hurtful experiences or the glory days. The past is gone. If you identify with those thoughts, you are living in an illusionary world. Sadness, anger, or hurt will accompany living in the past. The same is true if you allow your thoughts to take you to the future. This is also an illusionary world where negative feelings reside.

> With practice, you will be able to become your own counselor.

With practice, you will be able to become your own counselor. You will "see" your thoughts taking you to dysfunctional and negative places. You will know you are not your thoughts, let them go, and come back to the present moment.

You will create healthier thoughts and move toward a solution that will not include time on a couch.

Study Questions

1) Practice meditation for five minutes. How did you feel afterwards? Practice meditation for ten minutes. How did you feel afterwards?
2) Practice seeing your thoughts so you will respond—not react—to a situation.
3) Write down an ego thought in which you are having a hard time letting go. Write down a spiritual thought for that same situation. Practice living from that spiritual thought.

Chapter Ten
Use Healthy Coping Strategies

Seth, a thirty-six year-old, came into counseling with his thirty-three-year-old wife, Sarah. When Seth was a child, his father had worked for the railroad and was rarely home to provide emotional support for his family. Seth's father never attended his music or athletic events. Seth was emotionally hurt all through his childhood and adolescence. He never learned how to cope in a healthy way with these losses. He then married Sarah, who grew up in a home where mom and dad always argued. Sarah's father was a farmer so he coped with an unhealthy marriage by staying out in the fields for long hours. Sarah said that she was always sad and wanted dad home. Sarah never learned healthy ways to cope with the hostility she grew up with and the emotional absence of her father.

Seth and Sarah re-created this same scenario in their marriage. They had the normal stresses of money and children in their marriage. Seth copes with this in an unhealthy way by working long hours. He even took a second job because he believes they are always on the brink of bankruptcy. (I later learned that they are financially solvent.) This negative coping strategy by Seth triggers Sarah's old issues of her dad not being home. Her coping strategy is to throw herself into her children. When Seth tries to parent the children, Sarah always finds fault with him. This causes Seth to leave the house which causes Sarah to stay emotionally distant from her husband. The wheel of suffering goes around and around. Neither Sarah nor Seth woke up believing they would spin this wheel, but they did and this negatively affects their children. The children will learn unhealthy coping strategies like Seth and Sarah learned from their parents.

Many adults use unhealthy coping strategies. A forty-five-year-old who is afraid to face conflicts with his boss has anger built up inside of him. He doesn't resolve the conflicts so he copes with his anger by getting mad at his wife and children. Another adult is unhappy with his job. He makes good money and he believes he cannot leave because of the difficult economic times. He copes with his stressful job by drinking Scotch from the time he gets home. These adults don't have parents to ground them or other authority figures to give them consequences. So the negative coping strategies continue, until their spouses ask for a divorce.

Adults who use unhealthy coping strategies can end up marrying someone who also uses unhealthy coping strategies. This creates fireworks in a home and places many, many individuals and couples on my couch.

Here is a philosophy in which I wholeheartedly believe: no one wakes up in the morning and says to him or herself, "I am going to screw up my day." But, sadly, people make messes of their days over and over and over. Why? Because they use unhealthy coping strategies.

Every time you use unhealthy coping strategies, by definition, your life is going to become incrementally more dysfunctional. Running away from a problem does not count as exercise. The problem—the lesson—wants a resolution. Trust me, it has patience.

The key to staying off the therapist's couch is to use healthy coping strategies. Each of the previous chapters is about healthy coping strategies. If you resolve conflicts, as discussed in Chapter 2, you will create a more functional environment and be happier with others. If you let go and forgive, as discussed in Chapter 3, you will not harbor anger, sadness, and resentment, and will be able to live a lighter, happier life. If you accept what happens and are willing to have a Plan B, as discussed in Chapter 4, you will be less likely to be stressed and swim upstream in your life. If you parent yourself in a healthy way, as discussed

> Running away from a problem does not count as exercise.

in Chapter 5, you will make better decisions, delay gratification, and create a good life. If you get outside of yourself, as discussed in Chapter 6, you will de-power your ego, and be happier because you will be receiving love—because that is what you are giving out. If you practice being non-attached, as discussed in Chapter 7, you will see the forest from the trees, communicate more effectively, and suffer less. If you talk to someone, as discussed in Chapter 8, you will get things off your chest, vent emotions, possibly hear good solutions, and create needed community. If you see your thoughts and meditate, as discussed in Chapter 9, you will slow down psychologically and physiologically, feel more peaceful, and be in a mental state to make better decisions.

Having a sense of humor is a great coping strategy. (Read Chapter 11 on www.paradoxpete.com) Remember from Chapter 8 that the mind is the chief architect of your reality. When someone does something that could be viewed as negative, choose another way to think about it. Use humor to help you see how absurd that behavior is and laugh at it—laugh with it—which will help you stay positive and move on from the circumstance.

Exercise is another healthy coping strategy. I can't tell you how many male teenagers in my office I have advised to get a punching bag, shoot hoops, or go for a jog when they feel angry. Moving that emotional energy in a healthy way is much more beneficial than putting a hole in the wall or cussing and yelling at a family member.

Another form of exercise is the exercise of restraint, a coping strategy that helps a person wait to express something until an appropriate opportunity presents itself. I humorously reflect to teens that they exercise restraint by not farting in front of a person of the opposite sex. So they can exercise restraint by not back talking to a teacher, skipping a class, or swearing at their parents. They can complain all they want to their friends after school.

Research shows that attending church is a positive coping strategy. Being part of a church provides a sense of community. Participating in the activities associated with church life feels good and it provides meaning. Belonging does not mean learning dry disciplines and dogma, but celebrating the love, forgiveness, and joy that comes from connecting with God and others. These benefits have a high correlation with optimism, self-esteem, and more hardiness.

One of the teachings of all religions is forgiveness. Most people who come into my office are not practicing this coping strategy. Their egos are entrenched in the belief that someone else was wrong and should never be forgiven or that the other person should initiate the healing process. Usually, this is not going to happen. Freelance writer Robert Brault wrote, "Life becomes easier when you accept an apology you never got." This is a vital coping strategy if you want to stop suffering and stay off the therapist's couch.

Taking initiative is a coping skill that will get you far in life. Taking care of your business, checking off items on your to do list, and being responsible allows you to keep the power in your life. The opposite of this is being reactive. This means a boss, a parent, a spouse, or a friend will remind you, nag you, or even give you an ultimatum to get something done. In these circumstances, you have given your power to the other person. This feels negative, and might create another reactive behavior that could lead to deeper trouble.

Dr. Martin Seligman, a positive psychology psychologist, gave his students a task: Do one pleasurable activity and one philanthropic activity, then write about both. He wrote that, "The afterglow of the pleasurable activity paled in comparison with the effects of the kind action." This shows the benefits of getting outside yourself (Chapter 6) and caring for the wellbeing of someone or something else. Happiness is a side effect of making a meaningful contribution.

A client recently told me he plays the piano when he is stressed. He said based on his mood is how loud or soft he plays the songs on the piano. He stated that this is his favorite and most functional coping strategy.

Here's what is at stake if you don't learn and practice healthy coping strategies: your children will learn the unhealthy coping strategies that you are modeling. Rest assured, your children are watching you and they will copy the behaviors that they see. For example, a seven- year-old yells at his five-year-old sister: "If I've told you once, I've told you a thousand times, pick up your mess!" The seven-year-old learned two things from a parent. First, he learned these specific words. Second, he learned not to speak them but to yell them.

Adolescents are not as sophisticated in their unhealthy coping strategies as adults. So it is easier to see their mistakes. For example, when a class gets too difficult or the teen believes it's too boring, an unhealthy coping strategy is to skip the class. When the teen skips, he has escaped the unpleasant 50 minutes and feels good. Or, take a sixteen-year-old who feels she is not accepted by her peers because she doesn't drink alcohol. She doesn't like that feeling, so she decides to cope with the situation by drinking at the next party. She feels better that evening because people talked to her. Lastly, another teen has to listen to fights between her stepdad and mom almost every evening. She also was sexually abused by mom's previous boyfriend and she never reported the abuse. She is overwhelmed with emotional pain, so she starts cutting her arms with a razor blade. The physical pain overtakes the emotional pain so she feels better at that moment. In the short term, each teenager felt better by using an unhealthy coping strategy. This can reinforce similar dysfunctional actions in the future.

What happens to these adolescents if they keep using negative coping strategies? The teen who continues to skip class will only feel more stress because he is more likely to fall behind and flunk the classes. The sixteen-year-old who continues to drink alcohol will put herself at risk for getting busted by the police, getting in trouble with her parents, or may decide to drive her car home and create an even bigger problem. And the teen who cuts her arms can create permanent scars, and even commit suicide if she never talks about her problems.

None of these adolescents woke up and said they were going to royally screw up their days. Yet, they are all making their lives worse.

Teaching healthy coping strategies when grief issues occur is a major dynamic in counseling. Grief occurs whenever someone experiences a loss. The loss could be a job, a spouse through divorce, a child going off to college, realizing that your dad/mom were rarely there for you as a child, and the death of a loved one.

A negative coping strategy after suffering a loss is to "act strong" and not show any feelings. Whenever a loss occurs, feelings naturally follow. Remember, there is no escaping normal. You cannot escape the feelings of sadness, anger, fear, remorse, or guilt. If you don't express them, then you are stuffing them. This is called repression and whenever you repress something, in time, it will show itself, usually in a negative way.

A healthy coping strategy is to talk to someone (Chapter 8). Find a trusted person and express your feelings. Allow yourself to cry, or get mad,

Shrink-Proof Your Life

or be scared. You might feel exhausted afterwards, *and* you will feel lighter and better.

One definition of depression is anger turned inward. If you express your feelings of anger or sadness, the odds are that you will move that heavy energy out and feel lightness. This will move you further toward emotional health and you will stay off the therapist's couch and learn to be your own counselor.

Another unhealthy coping strategy is to ignore the emotional pain, thinking it will go away, or using drugs or alcohol to try and escape the pain. It is painful to have a pet die, lose a job, or have a best friend move to another city. You cannot escape the pain. You have to go through the pain. How? First, accept the loss (Chapter 4). Then, find a way to express the pain. This will move the pain from inside of you to something external. Some people journal. Others talk with someone, or paint, or plant a tree in honor of the person they have lost. Find your way. Use a healthy coping strategy.

Joining a support group can help you go through pain. Many people have not experienced your specific loss, so they don't know how to respond to your grief. For example, not everyone has had a miscarriage. They try to be helpful when they say, "You will have another baby." They don't understand that you wanted that baby. A support group of other moms who have experienced this loss, will more fully understand your grief, and then not make inappropriate comments.

In our culture, death is kept at arm's length and many people don't know how to *be* with someone who has experienced a death of a loved one. Jennifer was a 35-year-old client whose ten-year-old son had died of cancer. She was stuck in her pain two years after his death. One of Jennifer's comments that still rings in my ears is when she told me, "If someone says to me again, 'this was God's will,' I swear I will slap them."

I don't believe the people who said this wanted to harm Jennifer. But they did. Jennifer needed a support group of others who had experienced a similar loss. Jennifer needed to know she was not alone and she needed a place that was safe to talk about her pain. She needed people to love her, offer her hope, and be there for her when the pain overcame her.

Viktor Frankl wrote in *Man's Search for Meaning*, "...to live is to suffer, to survive is to find meaning in the suffering. If there is a purpose in life at all, there must be a purpose in suffering and in dying. But no man can tell another what this purpose is. Each must find out for himself, and must accept the responsibility that his answer prescribes."

In my office, I reflect a belief that is similar to Frankl's quote. I tell people that things don't happen *to* them, they happen *for* them. If you believe things happen to you, you will feel like a victim, use unhealthy coping strategies, and stay stuck in life. If you believe things happen for you, you will look for the life lesson—the meaning—and use healthy coping strategies to help you grow and become a more whole person.

You have to take your current mess and find the message to live a healthier and more joyful life. You have a difficult life. Your neighbor has a difficult life. This is normal. By implementing healthy coping strategies, you will be cultivating inner strength that will keep you off the therapist's couch.

Study Questions

1) How good are you at delaying gratification? How good are you at setting boundaries?
2) Which new healthy copying strategy do you want to start practicing?
3) Name an unhealthy coping strategy you are currently using? Do you see a reason to change your behavior and practice a healthy coping strategy? If so, adopt and practice a new one.

Epilogue

Everybody has either unconsciously or consciously answered Einstein's question about the nature of the Universe. Some live their life anxious and disturbed and do not know why and blame others or shame themselves. Others live their life more happy and peaceful and continue their conscious practice of trusting the Universe. We all need to answer this question consciously. There is no escaping normal.

If you believe the universe is friendly, it will be easier to:

- Name your issue, because you trust that you, or you with the help of others, or your Higher Being, will be able to resolve it. You actually believe the Universe is conspiring on your behalf.
- Resolve conflicts because you probably have surrounded yourself with others who also believe the Universe is friendly. You will trust each other and work toward what is best.
- Forgive and let go because you trust that the Universe is always working for what is best for you. You have no need to hold on to what is toxic or doesn't work anymore.
- Be more willing to accept what is and have a Plan B because you practice living the belief that the Universe is unfolding as it should.
- Parent yourself in a healthy way, because the Universe has modeled that to you.
- Get outside yourself because you have realized that when you have tried to trust only yourself and go it alone, you have always fallen short and lost your peace and happiness.
- Practice being non-attached because you know that suffering is not your true nature.

- Talk with someone about what is going on in your life. The Universe will actually bring you good people—not perfect—but good people who want to get outside themselves and listen to you.
- Practice meditation because you want to "see" if your thoughts are from your ego or from the friendly Universe. And,
- Practice healthy coping strategies because you want to align yourself with a Universe that knows what is best for you.

Your thoughts create your reality. "The Universe is friendly," is a thought. "The Universe is hostile," is a thought. "The Universe is both friendly and hostile," is a thought. Practice the ten tips and consciously lean into the thought, "The Universe is a friendly place."

English author and Anglican priest William Ralph Inge said, "Faith begins as an experiment and ends as an experience." You are creating an experiment and making a leap of faith that this book will help you be your own counselor. After practice and more practice, you will have experiences that are healthier and you will experience contentment. You will move from living in a melodrama to living in peace. This will take time. Be gentle with yourself. Rome wasn't built in a day. Your new and improved (and happier) life will be built each time you practice the truths from these ten chapters.

Buddha said, "In the end only three things matter: how much you loved, how gently you lived, and how gracefully you let go of things not meant for you." These are wonderful words which you understand with your mind. Practice and experience will allow you to truly know them in your heart.

Dag Hammarskjold, a Swedish diplomat who was the second United Nations Secretary-General and a Nobel Peace prize recipient said, "Each of us have been given sealed orders." You have incredible value. We need your gifts and talents. We need your "sealed orders." We need each other to evolve into our Better Selves? Will we? We'll see.

One of my favorite jokes I use in counseling sessions is this; how many therapists does it take to change a light bulb? One. But the light bulb has to want to change. You bought this book. You read this book. You are one of the "light bulbs" who wants to change.

If you walk through a field of grass, the first time you will not leave path. The blades of grass will go back to their original position. But if you walk through the field of grass the same direction for 21 days, you will have created a new path. The grass will bend to the consistency of the walking. Same is true for our neuropathways in our brain. If you try a practice one time, the neuropathways will bounce back to their habitual position. But if you practice consistency for 21 days, you will have created a new, healthy neuropathway in your brain.

Research shows that lasting change is accomplished by repetitive practices. Use smart phone technology to create a system of reminders of your new coping strategies. Create accountability with a friend or loved one about your new practices. Use web-based tools that provide step-by-step guidance. Write "The Universe is a friendly place" on a note and stick it on a bathroom mirror or a specific place at work. Even visit a therapist to help you further become your own therapist.

I leave you with three words: practice, practice, practice.

CPSIA information can be obtained at www.ICGtesting.com
Printed in the USA
LVOW08s1404201016

509590LV00001B/17/P